Stop Wishing. Stop Whining. Start Leading.

STOP WISHING. STOP WHINING. START LEADING.

A NO-NONSENSE, STRAIGHT-TALK GUIDE
FOR WOMEN WHO ASPIRE TO LEAD

Cynthia Kay & Doreen Bolhuis

ISBN: 1523303972
ISBN 13: 9781523303977
Library of Congress Control Number: 2016900335
CreateSpace Independent Publishing Platform
North Charleston, South Carolina

TABLE OF CONTENTS

INTRODUCTION

We wrote this book because of our sincere desire to share important information with women who aspire to lead. With over eighty years of combined experience in corporate and private business, we've learned many lessons in the "school of hard knocks." Starting our own businesses from scratch and running them successfully has taught us countless lessons—lessons learned only through such experiences. We don't pretend to know everything, but we do know much that will help other women in their own leadership journeys. We want to share information we believe is missing in many leadership books for women. After reading these books, we feel that too many criticize corporations for not doing enough for women instead of motivating women to stand up for themselves. They give women passes for not progressing to the upper levels of leadership and blame men for not doing more for women.

Our goal is very different. We want to add to the conversation, provoke women to think more deeply about their own leadership, and encourage women to take responsibility for their actions. Each woman is unique. Therefore, each woman's journey will be too. We aim for our experiences to help others find their way and fully utilize their talents and passions.

So, begin the journey now. Read on.

PART 1: SO, YOU WANT TO LEAD

CHAPTER 1

GIVE UP THE FAIRY TALE: IT'S UP TO YOU

S adly, we just read yet another article about what "needs to change" so that women can be successful leaders in business. This topic is a prevalent theme in books, articles, presentations, and discussions about women and leadership. However, we perceive this idea as a perpetuation of the fairy-tale philosophy that has historically disabled women and girls. Specifically, being dependent on others and the idea that a knight in shining armor will come along and save you. Nearly every Disney movie and fairy tale perpetuates this myth, and girls buy in to it at very early ages. Later, the deeply held dream is subtly at work in the psyche—even when a woman believes she's outgrown it. We see this myth at work in reality shows such as *The Bachelor* and *The Real Housewives*. The myth is still pervasive in our culture and even in many families. In those families, boys are challenged, and girls are given passes to be weak and fearful or to underperform. Girls are often protected by everyone around them to the extent that those girls don't practice and learn how to be brave, resilient, and self-reliant. As a result, women are often unknowingly disabled from reaching their true potential.

Think about it. Men generally don't expect everyone else to change or accommodate their special needs, wishes, and situations. Boys learn to be resilient and resourceful at an early age.

Watch any group of boys interact, and you will see them tease, embarrass, push, and continually jostle and compete for position. Boys learn to stand up for themselves, adapt to harsh conditions, and figure out how to get to the top. No one is protecting them. Boys are expected to stand on their own two feet, and thus they practice and learn how to do it.

For men, this early training carries over into their careers. Men face inevitable difficulties that accompany building their careers. They expect the journey to be difficult, and they don't complain when it is. Men just figure out ways to keep moving forward and keep moving up. Men don't start talking about how things need to change for them to succeed. By the way, not every man does succeed. That's part of the reality too. Not everyone becomes a CEO. Men accept these realities of the business world and expect to sacrifice and work hard to succeed. Men generally don't whine, complain, or talk about how companies need to change so they can succeed. Men usually don't blame the workplace or society or cite any number of other reasons why they can't get ahead. Instead, they network, talk to other professionals, increase their knowledge and competencies, let their supervisors know they want to move up, negotiate for pay increases, and utilize many other strategies we'll talk about in this book. Men keep adjusting their strategies and competing to achieve their goals. In contrast, many women complain and drop out when the challenges become tougher than they want to face.

Business is competitive and the climate is changing every day. Running a successful business is tough; we know because we've both established and successfully led businesses. There were certainly days when we wanted to quit—when we were tired, discouraged, scared, and overwhelmed. However, we didn't give up and are here to tell you that the sacrifices and struggles were worth the effort. Staying in it for the long haul has taught us to be tough. It's given us confidence, courage, and financial rewards too. We've become better people in the process because we've learned much more than if we hadn't chosen this adventure. Starting and running our own businesses has exposed us to financial risk, criticism, and even downright opposition, but we've become more courageous as a result. Because we had to figure out how to get over and under the many barriers in our way, we've become more resourceful, innovative, and creative. As business owners, the responsibility for our employees and customers has taught us to care for others. Leading every day as CEOs has taught us more leadership lessons than we can count. Looking back, we are proud of what we've achieved and whom we've become—though some days we wondered if it was really worth it. Our perseverance and commitment have benefited our companies and us. We endeavored to stay focused on what to do and how to do it versus what others needed to do for us. With long and successful careers behind us, we can say we are glad we chose our paths. We are glad we didn't drop out or give up.

Being business leaders, we know companies need people who are focused, hardworking, and invested in the company's success. Businesses everywhere offer valuable services and products. Companies provide salaries and benefits for employees and give back to their communities. To maintain a healthy business, the good of the whole must take precedence over an individual and his or her personal needs. This doesn't mean individuals don't matter. They certainly do. However, the company is not responsible for solving your personal challenges. That is your job. There are certainly as many personal problems and ways of solving them as there are people in the world. It is vital for business that people solve their problems and come to work prepared to contribute and help the company be successful. If you come to work expecting your company to accommodate your needs or provide what you need, you will simply not produce at the level of someone who is focused on what the company needs and how to help the business achieve its goals. Employees who are thinking about their own needs are liabilities rather than assets to the company. If you really do want to succeed, don't be one of those people! Check your attitude and gain a new and more powerful perspective.

So, for everyone—men and women—the question is not, "How is my company going to help me?" but rather, "How am I going to help myself?" Highly successful people already understand this concept, and those who hope to be successful must learn it. Learning to be successful means developing strategies to navigate the inevitable barriers that get in the way. Everyone faces barriers. Some people back down, give up, or give in to discouragement. Those who become successful see each roadblock as a challenge, and they find a way to move through or around each one. They do not give up until they figure out solutions—no matter how long it takes. Whether women face more barriers than men is not the most important question. The most important question is what to do to navigate around the barriers and take another step toward your goals.

For example, if you have children, how will you parent and also build your career? If someone at work is mean to you, how will you work around that person and continue to build your career? If you are denied a promotion at your company, how will you continue to move up the ladder and build your career? If your current company's culture does not promote women, how will you find a company that does? If you are currently underpaid, how will you negotiate for an increased salary? If you need new skills or leadership insights, how will you educate yourself? If you are stressed, overworked, frustrated, scared, confused, or angry, how will you overcome these challenges and develop strategies to move forward? If you need a support system, how will you find one?

Building a successful career is not easy, and there are many obstacles and challenges along the way for everyone—men and women. Women must accept what men already know—it will be hard, and no one will do it for them. In addition, men don't expect to do it all by themselves. They rely on multiple support systems. This includes personal assistants, business teams, business consultants and coaches, wives, girlfriends, extended family, neighbors, and so on.

Women often try to do everything themselves because they mistakenly believe they should. Frequently, women feel guilty for having personal assistants or asking family members to help them. They feel guilty for asking their children to help with chores. They feel guilty for assigning tasks to other team members, believing they need to do things themselves or control everything. Many women are too focused on the small details and lose the big picture. This causes stress for themselves and everyone around them in the process. When women realize they can't do it all themselves, they often drop out of working, start complaining that the playing field is not fair, or start talking about how companies need to help them. Women don't need to personally do it all. They just need to figure out how to get things done. Remember, no one knows your values, needs, and life situation better than you. No one is in a better position to solve your problems than you. How can you strategize for a company if you don't practice strategic thinking in your own life? Instead of talking about how things should change, build your personal power by taking responsibility for your own success, career, and future without expecting anyone else to do it for you.

Level Three Leaders (we'll talk more about this later) must be courageous, persevering, resilient, and strategic. These qualities are honed through hard work and years of practice facing challenges. Anyone who ultimately aspires to become a high-level leader cannot afford to drop out because you will never catch up to those who stayed in the business world and continued to build their skills and careers. It would be like starting a marathon a mile behind everyone else in the race. It's not possible to catch up—no matter how hard you try. Being first off the start line and running the entire race strategically is the way to win. Remember that your current life circumstances are usually temporary, and with a sound strategy, you can navigate through them. It might even mean working part time until your situation changes, but resist dropping out if you envision future professional success.

In summary, there are no fairy tales in business, and probably no one will come to save you. It is up to you to create the career you want that suits your goals and vision for your future. It is up to you to find the support and resources you will need. We hope the insights in this book will help you on your way.

Tips and Takeaways:

- Unlike boys, girls are often protected. As a result they don't practice and learn how to be brave, resilient, and self-reliant. They unknowingly buy in to the fairy tale that people will protect and save them.
- Women must take ownership of and responsibility for building their own careers.
- Dropping out of the workplace is not a good option. Women must stay in the work world to develop long and successful careers.

CHAPTER 2

UNSEEN BARRIERS: ARE YOU GETTING IN YOUR OWN WAY?

Today, there is certainly no lack of motivational speakers. These are the charismatic people who tell you that you can do anything. They hold seminars and sell you books and DVDs. They make it seem as if all you have to do is will yourself to be successful. They pump you up and get you really excited. In fact, encounters with these motivators can produce adrenaline and make you feel powerful. The problem is that the high is short lived and doesn't really take you anywhere. Success in your career is not about how you feel. It is about what you do or don't do; it's about attitude and action. Feeling empowered by a seminar or motivational speaker can be a great feeling. However, when the feeling fades, you still need to figure out what actions and strategies to implement to move forward. If you lack the tools and skills you need to take action, you can end up feeling discouraged and powerless. When this happens, women sometimes believe they don't have what it takes and give up. We, however, hope for women to become empowered to dream big and never give up on those dreams.

Unfortunately, in the workplace and at home, many women expect that others will care for them, watch out for them, and defend them. Many females have been raised to believe they need others to help them. When people don't step up to care for them, they blame those people. We have often heard women say they do much of the work, but their bosses or supervisors do not seem to notice or appreciate the effort. Women complain they don't get the plum assignments. Some say they are discriminated against when it comes to promotions. While there is certainly some evidence that women do not get equal pay for equal work, women do need to take responsibility for managing their own careers. Managing your own career means taking action to break through barriers—both real and perceived.

The simple truth is there are some legitimate reasons why women do not progress. There are unseen barriers we ourselves create. It's critical to understand these barriers and the strategies to navigate around them if you want to be a successful leader.

Barrier: women often do not dream big dreams.

Women sometimes set their sights on things they know are achievable instead of really thinking big. Perhaps it is a fear of failure or lack of confidence. Michelangelo wrote something we should keep in mind. He said, "The greatest danger for most of us is not that our aim is too high and we miss it, but that it is too low and we reach it." When we first enter the working world, we have dreams about where we want to go and what we want to achieve. So, what happens to our dreams? We start to listen to those around us who put roadblocks in the way. We work dutifully for those who might have no dreams of their own. We start to focus on the barriers to our dreams instead of making the dreams the focus. Before long, we get trapped in a job and depend on the income. We trade the dreams for paychecks. We lose our confidence and courage and settle for something less because it is safe, it is what we know, or it is what everyone else is doing. We lose our imagination, creativity, innovation, and joy when we give up our dreams.

Strategy to Overcome

The strategy for overcoming this is first to stop and remember why the dream was important. Ask yourself, "Is it still important?" It might not be. Perhaps your idea of a dream job has changed. Maybe what was once appealing is no longer desirable. If the dream is still important, what is the need or driving force behind it? Do you want to prove yourself? Do you need a challenge? Do you want to hold power? Do you want control? If the dream is still important, you need a strategy. Think of it this way—if you set off on any journey, you decide on your destination first. After that, you plan your route. You already understand this process and can use it in planning your career and future. Here is what that process might look like as you plan to achieve your dreams and goals.

Ask yourself:

- What is your destination? Is it full time or part time? Is it management level, executive level, or some other position? What industry, size of company, and lifestyle do you envision? Do you aspire to own a company?
- What are the possible routes to achieve your goals? Will you take a direct route to the top or some side roads to enjoy the journey? Are achievement and position most important to you, or are flexibility and control over your lifestyle paramount? Do you prefer small business or corporate America?
- What is the time line? Are you taking the scenic route or the fast track? Do you want to be an executive when you are thirty, forty, fifty, or sixty? If you will need further education, what is the time line for this?

- What skills/education/experiences do you need that you currently do not possess? What institution or program will you choose for your training or education, and when will you complete this? How long do you want to work?

The questions above are simply some samples to get you started. As you answer them, you will have the beginning of a strategy to build your career and future. A sound planning process for your journey will empower you to make intentional choices and recognize opportunities to reach your ultimate destination.

Barrier: women are often internally focused.

Women are sometimes more concerned about how they feel and look than what is going on around them. Women can often tell you exactly how the actions of others in the workplace have affected them. They are less likely to step outside of themselves to understand others' perspectives. This perspective is self-focused rather than being strategically focused on how to move a team or company forward. Additionally, it results in taking things very personally which clouds a leader's judgment. Success in business is not about how you personally feel. Career success is about transcending feelings to focus on what you need to do.

Strategy to Overcome

Stop thinking about yourself, and start being a problem solver. The hard truth is that your boss is usually not thinking about you or your career. He or she is concerned about the entire organization—not one individual. It is important to understand how people respond to what is new, what is creative, and what is producing results. These things help move an organization forward. So, do more than just bring problems to the table. Bring solutions. We strongly advise women to be part of the solution—not part of the problem. Begin to look at what is going on around you through the lens of others rather than how you are personally affected.

Barrier: women often lack the confidence to compete.

Over the years, we have watched women sit back and not even try to get promotions or places at the table. When you ask them why, it becomes obvious they do not have the confidence in themselves to try. Even women who seem self-confident admit they often fake it. They can talk a good game, but inside little voices are telling them they are not good enough, smart enough, or tough enough to compete. How does this happen? We believe it starts at a very young age. Everyone has fears about something. The fears of girls and boys may be very similar but many parents respond to daughters very differently than their sons. When a boy expresses fear, he is pushed to act and "man up." When a girl expresses fear, she often gets a pass. Girls are not pushed to be courageous and are thus denied the practice of facing fears that they need to develop self-confidence.

Strategy to Overcome

There is an amazing technique called self-talk. Counselors employ this when working with individuals who have anxiety and fear in certain situations. It works like this. You ask yourself, "What is the worst thing that can happen if I do (x)?" You play out the scenario, and most people discover that the worst thing is really not that bad. You realize you can face your fear and cope with situations that don't turn out the way you planned. When you feel a lack of confidence, realize that confidence comes from something very real. It comes from ability. As you increase your ability in any area, greater confidence comes with it. This might mean you need to take action to increase your ability. The worst thing that can happen is you fail, and this won't kill you. In fact, we all learn more from our greatest failures than from our greatest successes. In this world that is so focused on success, we have forgotten that the most successful people have failed many times, picked themselves up, and tried again. As Winston Churchill said, "Success is not final, failure is not fatal: it is the courage to continue that counts." Avoiding situations or not acting does not help you progress. It is critically important to be active rather than passive because the active people will pass you by if you are passive. Start with a small challenge and work up to bigger ones. You will become stronger and more confident as you face your fears and act despite them.

Barrier: women often fade into the background.

When a woman achieves something of great value, she will often downplay it. In contrast, when men achieve things, they take credit for them. Women will talk about those who helped them or supported them or say they were lucky or that they worked really hard. They essentially fade away because they don't want to stand out and take credit. There is an award in our area sponsored by the *Grand Rapids Business Journal* that recognizes the fifty most influential women every other year. For many years, the editor said they had to beg and cajole women to apply. Most simply do not think they are influential, or they do not want to appear to be bragging. They prefer to simply fade into the background.

Strategy to Overcome

Do your homework or research so you become an expert at what you do. Take every opportunity to learn from those around you, and put yourself in situations where you can make a contribution. Then raise your hand. Speak up. It might be uncomfortable when you first try this, but it gets easier over time. Be intentional about serving on boards and competing for awards. Set a goal that you will participate not to call attention to yourself but to add value. Prepare to ask a question that sparks thoughtful discussion. You don't need to know all the answers. You do need to ask powerful questions—questions that provoke others to think more deeply.

For example, Doreen was asked to sit on a regional board. After looking at the members of the board, it was obvious to her these were some of the most powerful professionals not only in the community but on the state and national levels. Doreen's goal was to contribute value rather than simply be a possible token female business owner. This board had been together for a significant period of time and knew the issues more thoroughly than she did. Her strategy was to research, listen, and then ask one important and provocative question to challenge the group to dive deeper into the issues that were on the agenda. It did not take long until the group members were looking to her to comment on or question the actions of the group. Those who had not known her or thought she was simply taking up room at the table saw the value she could bring to the organization.

Cynthia has had similar experiences. She stepped up to show support for the expansion of health-care benefits in Michigan by agreeing to speak at a press conference with Governor Rick Snyder. As a result, she has been called upon by local and national media to discuss the rising cost of health care. In fact, she was featured in *TIME* magazine. Both these examples illustrate that if you want a place at the table, you must take it by courageously speaking, contributing, and adding value. Forget fear and focus on how to help your company or board.

Barrier: women don't believe in themselves or promote their ideas.

Women are smart. They have unique perspectives. They possess outstanding talents. The problem is they don't believe in themselves. When a woman can clearly see the answer to a problem, she doesn't step forward and offer it. Women believe everyone else can already see it, and they don't believe their unique perspectives have value. Because they believe everyone else has the answer, women don't step forward or raise their hands. They wait for someone else to solve the problem. When women hesitate, they get left in the dust by others (usually men) who do step forward to offer their ideas. Leading necessarily means stepping forward—even if it feels like a risk. Leaders take initiative because they are more focused on the good of the whole than themselves individually.

Strategy to Overcome

Step out and lead. Take on an important project. Propose a solution. Ask critical questions that provoke a group to deeper thinking. Address the elephant in the room (diplomatically). Be involved every day in finding and proposing solutions for your company. Understand that no one will hand you opportunities, so don't wait to be asked. It is your responsibility to take initiative. In Cynthia's book *Small Business for Big Thinkers*, she talks about the importance of positioning yourself. Once you have taken the lead on a project and accomplished something, you need to take the next step. Brag about it—tastefully, of course. In the book, Cynthia writes, "So often we are raised to be humble, not to brag about accomplishments, not to go for the awards. But recognition is important if you want to be known as an expert in your field. And, who doesn't want that? After all, no one wants to work with someone who is just average."

Barrier: women tend to worry more than men.

Many of the women we know are worriers. They worry about their families, their children, and their friends. At work, they worry about the quality of their work, how they are being perceived, and so much more. When women worry, it can paralyze them and be a barrier to success. Worry also means you are not thinking about strategies and initiatives because you are overly focused on the problem. Worry is counterproductive rather than productive.

Strategy to Overcome

In Daniel Amen's book *Unleash the Power of the Female Brain,* it says that, "Women have busier brains which when connected with their associative thinking powers, helps identify problems sooner and create solutions." This ability can be a real advantage for women in their careers if leveraged correctly. One strategy is to fix what is worrying you. Be like a horse with blinders on. Filter out any distractions and analyze the problem's source. Don't make it larger than it is, and don't let worry derail you and your actions. Instead, let your concern be the fuel that drives you to solve the problem. Stay focused and create solutions instead of wasting time worrying. We know of one woman who sets aside time every day to worry. It might sound silly, but she has disciplined herself to take that time to worry. When the time is up, she moves on. Practice putting worries in perspective so you become a positive problem solver instead of letting fear paralyze you. Focus instead on the things you have control over. It will empower you.

Barrier: women do not put themselves in places where they can network and excel.

Women sometimes think they need to connect with and build their networks with other women and shy away from opportunities to network with powerful businesspeople of both sexes. They go to places and events where they are comfortable—even if there are no apparent benefits.

Strategy to Overcome

Avoid joining exclusively women's organizations, and stop joining any organization where you are not challenged or inspired. Get uncomfortable. That means you are growing. Look at organizations that can help you get to where you need to be. This means you need to think strategically. Look at the list of board members and also the members of potential organizations. Are these people who can help you broaden your knowledge, make business connections, and challenge you? What does the organization provide in terms of programming opportunities, speakers you might not otherwise hear, or seminars that help you solve business issues? Is there an opportunity for you to play a leadership role in the organization? One more thought. Don't be confined by geographic barriers. Look beyond your local chamber or business group. Look across the state. Look at national organizations. Bottom line—choose experiences that force you to grow and step up your game.

One example of this can be found in Cynthia's efforts to advocate for small business. She began by looking beyond her local chamber to statewide organizations. She joined the Board of the Small Business Association of Michigan and worked her way up to chair of the board. Today she serves on the National Small Business Association and is advocating for small business on the national level.

Doreen stepped out and used her network to gain a recommendation for the Governor's Council on Physical Fitness, Health and Sports. She now sits on this statewide board and also on the Michigan Fitness Foundation Board. Resist placing limitations on yourself, and reach beyond your perceived limits.

Barrier: women tend to put limits on how long they want to work and what type of benefits they need.

It is true that even today women are the primary caregivers and managers of their homes. They often want regular schedules so they can be available for family. As a result, women limit their opportunities because it is difficult to juggle home and work. Women also limit themselves by not being as strategic about career moves or taking opportunities.

Strategy to Overcome

Start with a clean slate. Throw out your old limitations. Stop thinking, "I have to be off every day at five. I need to have a job with flexible hours. I can't work on Saturday." Start to think of your career as a game of Chutes and Ladders. You need to take some risks. You need to look at opportunities that will get you to where you want to be. That might mean you have to take a job for a while that does not have the flexibility you want or the hours you need. The bigger question is whether it will get you to the next level. Then you have to ask yourself if the next level is a place where you want to be.

Doreen is a great example of how an educator and mother of two took a risk and started her own business. She could have kept teaching and working regular hours with summers off. Instead, she created Gymco, Inc., a sport and recreational facility that has served over one hundred thousand children since it opened its doors in 1980. Like all small business owners and leaders, she did not shy away from doing the hard work to make her vision a reality. In this case, it meant lots of hours after school and on weekends—when most children and families have time for recreation. However, she knew she would need to juggle her personal and professional lives. She was strategic in planning time for both work and family and put support systems in place as needed. She was all in, and today she owns her own award-winning facility and employs thirty people.

Barrier: women do not advocate for themselves and negotiate for pay and position.

Women hope someone will notice if they work hard instead of making sure they are noticed. They work hard, keep their heads down, and wait for promotions. They labor tirelessly and quietly. As a result, they might end up with less pay and be passed over for promotions.

Strategy to Overcome

Take the time to write down all the things you have done that have brought results to your organization. This can be things you have done alone or as part of a team. Be specific. Wherever possible, use measurable results. Do not wait for that one right moment to advocate for yourself. There is no perfect moment. Instead, you must use every opportunity to position yourself. Set a time line for having important conversations about your future with your organization. One important thing to know is that most conversations about your career will take place when you are not even in the room. However, you can be in control of what is being said about you if you are strategic about consistently contributing ideas, getting results, and communicating your value in timely and appropriate ways.

Barrier: women tend to play right into the stereotypes they condemn.

To be sure, there are many stereotypes of female leaders. There is the bossy or bitchy leader, and there are women who fall apart or cry under pressure. Are women unfairly stereotyped? Maybe so. Maybe not. There is no doubt though, there is a distinct difference in the words we use to describe female leaders as opposed to male. However, women sometimes reinforce these stereotypes without even knowing it. They react to situations instead of communicating in a proactive and clear manner. Women frequently use too many words and too much emotion.

Strategy to Overcome

We will talk more about this in What Not to Do, but in short, we all create our own reputations. Everything you do contributes to making your mark as an individual. You cannot break down every stereotype. So, stop reacting when people call you bossy or some other adjective you don't like. You do not need to behave like a man, but you must be a consistent, calm, disciplined leader and set your own pace. You also need to be strategic and thoughtful about everything you say and do because your actions will build your reputation. A final tip: if you don't want something repeated, then don't say it. It is easy to get caught up in the moment and blurt out something that can come back to haunt you. This is especially true in this day and age where cell phones capture video—even when you do not know you are being recorded.

Barrier: women do not have the same economic standing as men.

Many women today bear the burden of being single parents responsible for the support of children. Some women support partners who have lost jobs and been unable to find employment or are unable to work. In addition to these challenges, there is a great deal of evidence that women do not get equal pay for equal work. As a result, they can be economically disadvantaged.

Strategy to Overcome

Overcoming economic barriers is a complex topic, and there is no simple solution. Education or retraining is one way to begin the process. However, women need to proceed carefully here. Often women choose traditional careers instead of looking at what jobs are most likely to provide them with great incomes. A college education is not always a requirement. Many certificate and training programs take less time, and starting salaries are attractive. Some programs might offer paid internships while going to school. It is important to consider your economic future when choosing your career path to position yourself for future financial success.

Look at what programs your current employer has for tuition reimbursement. That can help reduce the cost of your education. However, you might need to commit to staying on the job for a period of time. There are also funds available in many states to help unemployed workers train for jobs with local companies. Plan your career by thinking about earning potential in addition to your passion and talent.

Barrier: women encounter gender bias within their organizations or from supervisors.

It might be subtle, but it exists. There are companies and men in power that simply do not value women. In these companies, there are few women in the ranks of middle management. Women who are there seem to be stalled and do not rise to positions of significant leadership. The environment is not female friendly, and the culture might have condescending undertones or even be openly hostile.

Strategy to Overcome

Before you are tempted to blame an organization, first look inward. Are you making assumptions about the organization that might not be true? Are you really putting yourself out there, or are you expecting someone will notice your good work? One thing you need to do is separate what you perceive to be true and what is really true. Look at what supervisors say and do. Do you notice gender-biased language? Do you see signs of behavior that is deferential to men?

If you believe there is a gender bias, then you need to make some difficult decisions. Do you pursue action through the company? Do you have enough clear evidence to bring this to the attention of the human resources department? This will take some time, effort, and risk. Should you simply move on to an organization where there are greater opportunities for you? This is a very individual choice, and you might want to get input from others about this decision before making it.

While this is not an exhaustive list of unseen barriers for women, it does provide insights into common barriers women face. Women create some of the barriers themselves. Others exist because of the actions or perceptions of individuals and organizations. One thing should be noted—women are not the only ones who face unseen barriers. Men also must navigate roadblocks. However, they are sometimes different ones than women face. When you understand the barriers, you can develop strategies to overcome them and become the leader you want to be.

Exercise: Break Down Your Barriers

Write down the one or two main barriers to achieving your goal to lead. The barriers can be the ones noted above or a unique one that you face. Answer these questions:

- When did this barrier begin?
- Is this a barrier that I created or does it exist because of an individual or organization?

- Who can assist me with developing a strategy to overcome this barrier?
- How likely am I to succeed?
- What specific actions do I need to take?

Once you have completed this task, put the answers away for a few days. Come back and review them with fresh eyes. If the insights and strategies still appear to be appropriate, discuss them with a leader you respect, mentor or coach. Then act.

Tips and Takeaways:

- Managing your career means taking action to break through barriers—both real and perceived.
- There are legitimate reasons why women do not progress, and women create some of the very barriers they must overcome.
- You must analyze and understand the barriers to create strategies to navigate them and become a successful leader.

CHAPTER 3

THREE LEVELS OF LEADERSHIP

Despite all the literature, articles, seminars, and attention heaped upon leaders, we think there is very little understanding about what leadership is and the different levels of leadership.

There are a number of books that describe the three levels of leadership model. In this chapter we will describe our own three levels of leadership for women based upon our experience and how women can move from one level to another.

First, there is a difference between a boss and a leader. A boss is someone who people have to follow. You generally do not get a lot of choice about your boss. Others decide that. You are simply told this person or that person will be your boss and you will report to him or her. While some bosses are better than others, most, if they think of themselves as "bosses," have hierarchical views of their work. They make the decisions and pass them on and you follow.

A leader, on the other hand, is someone who people choose to follow. Why? There are some very good reasons and some common misperceptions. One misperception is that leadership has a lot to do with money. Many assume those who lead are at the top earning levels. They believe leadership and money are closely tied together. Nothing could be further from the truth. Many top earners are not good leaders.

Leadership is also not about being the smartest person. That is not to say leaders are not smart. They are. However, being smart does not guarantee one can lead. Smart people might create all kinds of products and programs. A leader knows how to leverage the knowledge of all team members and create something far better than the output of one person.

Leaders are not bullies. They do not intimidate people who work for them to try to get them to act in certain ways or follow them. They never threaten.

Good leaders are also not commanders. They do not tell people what to do but rather encourage creativity, problem solving, and initiative. They guide—not command.

Leadership is not about a title. Look around any business today at individual supervisors, vice presidents, or C-suite executives. Just having the title does not mean that person has the vision or experience to lead a department or organization. Sometimes individuals reach these levels because they have longevity. They were simply the next people in line. People promoted beyond their levels of leadership due to timing and circumstances might find themselves in places they do not want to be.

Good leaders are not arrogant or self-important. They know their strengths and are realistic about their skills, but they do not throw their knowledge or accomplishments in the faces of others.

Good leaders do not take credit for what others have done in an effort to elevate themselves. This is a common complaint we hear from employees. They say they do not get the credit or visibility for having done the work because their leaders claim the credit.

Well-known authors and leadership experts Barry Z. Posner and James M. Kouzes have a program many corporations and organizations use. According to the back covers of their books,

The Leadership Challenge and *The Student Leadership Challenge* "demonstrate how anyone can be a leader, regardless of age or experience." Posner and Kouzes illustrate what they call the Five Practices of Exemplary Leadership®:

- Model the Way
- Inspire a Shared Vision
- Challenge the Process
- Enable Others to Act
- Encourage the Heart

There is no doubt these practices have helped many become great leaders. However, we believe there is more to it than that. We don't believe every person can be a good leader. We think there are three very distinct levels of leadership. We will define these for the sake of simplicity as Level One, Level Two, and Level Three. Not everyone can become what we define as a Level Three Leader. It takes hard work and years of practice, and we think there are some innate qualities that set Level Three Leaders apart. This chapter will help you assess where you are now and the leadership level to which you aspire.

Great leaders progress through all the leadership levels, but some might do it more quickly than others. You will learn important and necessary lessons at each level that will help you advance and become more successful at higher levels of leadership.

Level One—The Foundation

As with any skill you want to achieve, you must build a foundation. Pianists learn to play scales before they play nocturnes. Athletes learn basic throwing and catching before they become accomplished baseball players. You need to learn basic math before you can tackle calculus.

So, how do you build a foundation for leadership? Foundationally, leaders live their lives in responsible ways. That means they understand they are responsible to themselves and their family, friends, and communities. They organize and prioritize their personal lives to best fulfill their responsibilities, which is visible in some of the following realms. Read the descriptions to see if you recognize yourself as a potential leader.

Finances

You understand how to budget. You never spend more than you make. You pay bills on time and have some left over for savings and investments. You understand the consequences of making large purchases (such as a home) or investments (such as a business start-up or expansion costs) and plan for them.

Schedule

You know how to manage your time. You follow through on commitments and deliver what you promise on schedule. You are not overcommitted and scattered. You arrive on time. People trust that they can depend on you. If you find yourself apologizing to people frequently, you need to work on skills in this area.

Environment

These are the places where you live and work. Your environment affects your ability to think, your stress level, and your ability to be efficient. In order to be successful, your environment is organized so you can find what you need when you need to get work done. You have the tools you need and have minimized distractions. You have created systems that work for you.

Relationships

A good leader has personal and professional relationships with individuals whom they can trust and depend upon. They are positive relationships where there is mutual give-and-take. You are not held hostage by relationships that require you to constantly save others. You do not hold grudges but work out issues in a mature, open, and healthy manner. You are able to tell others what you need from them and are able to respond when they ask you for reasonable things.

Addictions

You are free from addictions and obsessive behavior.

When your life is in order, others begin to view you as a role model. People seek you out to help solve their problems. You are a positive influence wherever you are and whatever you are doing. Leaders at this level often give back by volunteering time and talent. However, they know how to set boundaries and hold themselves and others accountable to work within those boundaries. They are intentional about doing the work without letting others take advantage of them.

Level One Leaders might or might not have titles, but people do respond to them as leaders—even though they might not yet see themselves in that light. This is a solid foundation to build upon.

Level Two—A Work in Progress

More intentional and active engagement in leadership characterize this level. You begin to eagerly anticipate a higher level of responsibility. You feel compelled to move up. To do that, you understand and take seriously the need for more education. You look for leadership development opportunities that will provide the knowledge and skills it takes to get the job done.

The focus starts to shift from the immediate world around you to a larger perimeter. You start to understand systems thinking. You take steps to reach outside your area of work and expertise to learn about your greater organization because you know a complete understanding of the workplace is needed. You start to see the bigger picture.

At this level, leaders might be moved into supervisory capacities or be invited to participate in higher-level activities outside their immediate responsibilities. As you take on new roles and responsibilities, you are energized because you are able to help set direction. You are willing to sacrifice for leadership endeavors without feeling bad or guilty. This is because the work aligns with your values and mission.

Examples of leadership at this level can vary from chairing a committee at work to leading a new initiative or nonprofit effort.

Level Two Leaders carry more responsibility and are more intentional about leading. They enjoy the challenge of leadership. Another thing to note is that Level Two Leaders who aspire to progress to the next level must consistently move forward and continue to build their skills and careers. As previously mentioned, it is like training for a race with the goal of being first off the start line and running the entire race strategically to win and move up to the next level of competition.

Level Three—Executive Level

At this level, leaders are literally at the top of their game. These character qualities are honed through hard work and years of practice facing challenges. These individuals have had extensive experience. They have worked up to be CEOs or C-suite executives and often have been in their chosen fields for fifteen to twenty years or more.

Level Three Leaders might own businesses or be serial entrepreneurs. As a result, they are forward thinking and visionary. Once they have set their priorities, Level Three Leaders are all in. They approach their work or missions without any reservations. This type of leader does whatever it takes to get the job done. They do not resent all the effort this requires. This is not to say they are single minded. In fact, they are proactive about creating the best possible work-life balances.

Level Three Leaders are courageous when it comes to making decisions. They do not float ideas to get reactions. They make decisions based upon thoughtful research, the input of others, and their experience. It also goes without saying that they are not afraid to make the tough decisions. Those decisions might make them unpopular, but they are most concerned with what is best for their organizations.

Level Three Leaders also choose to take hits to protect others in their organizations. If someone has made a bad decision, a Level Three Leader does not abandon that person to suffer the consequences. He or she steps up and takes the responsibility—even though that leader might not have made the decision.

In these media-intense times, everything is under scrutiny. A company's actions or leaders are often criticized publicly using multiple channels. This includes social media. Leaders must shoulder the criticism for their organizations. When disasters occur, as they are bound to, the leader's actions can mean the difference between an organization's survival and demise.

Level Three Leaders are more concerned about building their companies and organizations than they are about promoting or elevating themselves. When Mary Barra was named CEO of General Motors in 2014, she probably had no idea how courageous she would need to be. When the company recalled eight hundred thousand small cars for faulty ignition switches, Barra had to testify before the House subcommittee and face the victims' families. Barra's leadership accelerated finding a solution and working with families of those who had died. She was not worrying about herself or preserving her position. She was concerned about caring for those who were wronged and moving her company past the crisis.

In 2015, Marissa Mayer, CEO of Yahoo, came under fire following the company's lavish holiday party which many believed was not appropriate given the company's financial situation. While the actual cost of the holiday party varied from source to source, even at the low end of the spectrum, it was a hefty price tag. As a leader, Ms. Mayer was called into question for not having good judgment about the cost to shareholders at a critical time for the company. As the company's leader, she had to answer for this decision and take the heat of public criticism.

Level Three Leaders are tough and resilient. This is not a level for the faint of heart. Level Three Leaders can handle the stress and weather the storms that inevitably accompany this level of leadership. They have inner strength and resiliency that empower them to lead at the highest levels.

Choosing Your Level of Leadership

Good leadership is a development process. It is a mistake to believe that people can skip from Level One to Three...or just magically be a Level Three. Many people begin this journey when they are children. On the playground, even at an early age, a leader is organizing, protecting others, helping, and giving back. Leadership truly is a development process, and there is nothing that can take the place of practicing the skills and learning from mistakes.

Many people aspire to be leaders, but we think the wise person is mindful of the levels, effort, and personal costs associated with each. You must choose a path and then be willing to do what is required to be the best at your chosen level. It's also important to note that you might choose different leadership levels at different times of your life.

You might be a Level Three while you are at the height of your career and then decide to drop back. You might have retired and want to be involved but also have more leisure time. You might be a Level Two single parent who chooses not to go to Level Three at this time so you can devote more time to family. No level is better than another. You need to find your own unique path as you consider the levels and what is appropriate for where you are in your life.

The bottom line is this—everything in life is about choices, and leadership is no exception. Great leaders know the reasons behind their choices and act in ways that support their values and help them achieve their goals.

Tips and Takeaways:

- There are three basic levels of leadership. Level One is the foundation. Level Two is a work in progress. Level Three is the executive level.
- You should build leadership skills progressively to create a strong foundation.
- Leadership level and commitment are choices. You should, therefore, weigh the costs and benefits.

CHAPTER 4

Administrative Assistant, Manager, or Executive: It Is a Choice

Determining the right fit for your leadership level and job responsibilities requires thoughtful planning, and your choices might change in different stages of your life and personal development. In fact, we know several women who began their careers as secretaries and ultimately became CEOs. We also know many who have chosen to continue in secretarial or administrative positions because those jobs fit their talents, passions, and lifestyles. You can obviously be a leader regardless of your title, but higher-level positions will carry greater responsibility and longer work hours and require more highly developed leadership skills. This chapter will help you better understand job realms and responsibilities to discern what is best for you now and in the future.

We know that women who have progressed all the way from administrative assistant positions to CEOs have gained tremendous value and insights from their journeys. It helped them understand the inner workings of companies in ways only gained through personal experience. These women know how to build systems and processes and communicate with people. They know how to manage projects. They are in touch with customers and employees and understand their needs. Whatever jobs women hold during their career paths, each and every one provides valuable insights for those who eventually do become CEOs. These experiences empower them to connect initiatives with the needs of customers and employees. It helps them understand the big picture and how the pieces and parts are interconnected. Working from the entry level to the top increases a female CEO's effectiveness because she is not working in a vacuum. This can happen to many CEOs who have not had these experiences.

As you learn about the job responsibilities in this chapter, evaluate yourself to see which one (or ones) best fit your talents and interests. We realize there are endless job titles, levels, and responsibilities in companies throughout the world, and we can't possibly cover them all. We've chosen three very common job functions for the sake of illustration and to keep things simple. Consider these different levels as you think about and plan your career path.

Administrative Assistant

An administrative assistant is at the heart of an organization. The most important talent required for this job is excellent organizational ability. An administrative assistant is responsible for processing, organizing, and communicating in the organization. An administrative assistant is able to multitask (handle many things simultaneously) and can hold unfinished tasks in mind while attending to emergencies and urgent matters. He or she seems never to drop the ball and can pick up loose ends for everyone else and tie them all together skillfully. Administrative assistants seem to do this with ease, and everyone turns to them when there is an emergency because they can figure out solutions so quickly. Their problem-solving abilities are superior, and they are usually involved in solving problems all day long. These are true gifts that every successful administrative assistant possesses. An excellent administrative assistant provides a critical foundation for teams and executives. Administrative assistants love organizing things because they are good at it. Organizing comes naturally to them, and they tend to organize and develop streamlined systems at work, at home, for friends, and in the organizations where they volunteer. They just can't stop. For talented administrative assistants, organizing is their heart, soul, and passion. They are happiest when creating order, and they gain great satisfaction by making positive differences in the world with their systems thinking.

If you recognize yourself in this description, think about whether you wish to remain in administrative work throughout your career or use it as a stepping-stone to get to the next level. The skills and experience will most certainly be assets as you move up the career ladder or start your own business. An administrative assistant's job schedule is generally predictable. This means an administrative assistant often has predetermined hours and can go home at the end of the day without needing to worry about what is happening in the organization when he or she is away. This is an advantage for professionals who are parenting or have other responsibilities after normal work hours. Administrative assistants can sometimes work part time for smaller companies or job-share with other administrative assistants. This makes their schedules even more flexible.

Manager

The main job responsibility of managers is working with people. Managers should love people because they are working with them all day long. They are working with their teams to provide the horsepower to get things done for their companies. They engage in strategic planning to achieve company objectives through the work of their departments and teams. Managers are responsible for training and coaching employees and monitoring their performances to maximize their potential. They assist staff with problem solving and systems development, and they conduct performance reviews. Managers formulate department policies and practices to maximize efficiency and productivity. They review financials for sales and performance. Managers have a wide variety of job responsibilities and are essentially jacks-of-all-trades. The management level requires excellent skills in communication, organization, judgment, decision-making, information management, resource management, human resources, problem solving, coaching, and teamwork. Great managers are leaders of people. They enjoy teaching, coaching, communicating, and helping their direct reports achieve their goals. The best managers are not only savvy in business but are also cheerleaders and supporters of the employees who are making business happen. Ideally, they have positive attitudes and are flexible while they help solve problems and develop great talent.

The training and experience you gain at the management level will broaden your scope of skills and challenge you to use more complex and strategic thinking. It will also help you understand the power behind any organization—its people. No organization can be great without great people, and managers are the ones who develop and support the important lifeblood of companies—their staffs. The relationships between managers and their teams are critical. Research shows that the quality of a relationship with a manager affects the enjoyment of an employee's work life. If a relationship with a supervisor is negative or stressful, a person will leave the job—even if that person likes the company and the product or service. Surprisingly, productive employees with great attitudes leave much faster than less productive employees with negative attitudes. This is because positive employees can get jobs at great companies with healthy cultures and skilled managers. You can see that companies depend on managers and that skilled managers are critical to business success.

Many managers are salaried, and as such, they might be required to work after hours or even on weekends. They often are called on at home if emergencies arise. The management level requires a deeper commitment than the administrative assistant level and is usually full time. Consider the management level when you can make a greater commitment to your work life and can manage an increased level of job stress. The management level will help you develop higher-level skills and a deeper understanding of the components of business success. It will also challenge you to develop your leadership skills more fully. As a manager, you might have many frustrating moments when you don't achieve the results you want from your teams and people. These are your best learning opportunities. You can figure out what works and utilize some of this book's information about great leadership. With practice you will improve! If you desire to move up to the executive level, management experience is an important step and one where you must first achieve success.

Executive

There is a common misconception that the job of CEO (or other executive) is one of privilege, but nothing could be further from the truth. An executive's job is primarily about responsibility. There might be some perks along with higher pay in an executive job, but that is because of the higher demand on time and commitment at this level. The skill qualifications required for executives are more stringent and take many years of education and experience to achieve.

Whether a vice president, president, or C-suite position (CEO, CFO, COO, etc.), an executive is responsible for oversight and strategic planning in the company. An executive must create vision and direction for the company and be skilled in strategic thinking. Executives do this by monitoring market conditions, economic climate, trends, cultural shifts, and a host of other factors that affect business in general and their companies specifically. In large corporations, executives are ultimately responsible to the boards of directors for keeping the companies healthy and profitable. They are responsible for the companies' public images, and they represent the faces of the companies to the public and the boards. Executives carry the burden of responsibility for excellence in every area of company performance. The buck stops with them, and executives must answer to their boards if the companies are underperforming.

For CEOs who own their companies, the burden is even greater because the stakes are higher. Business owners are personally financially invested in their companies and place their personal financial futures at risk should the companies fail. Business owners who have employees might feel even greater burdens of responsibility because they are likely the only executive officer. Without the support of teams of executive officers and managers, business owners fill every role from custodians to human resources to CEOs. They typically put in long hours over many years to build and maintain their companies. It is interesting that the number of female business owners is growing every year. Business ownership is an attractive option for women who aspire to be executives and also want some control over their lives. An advantage of owning your own business is that you can shape the culture and environment to fit your values. This is appealing to many women (and men) who have worked in large corporate businesses that are cutthroat and competitive. We can say from experience it is rewarding to create and maintain a workplace you and others enjoy and where you can create your own vision of success.

An executive must be a strategic thinker, problem solver, visionary, risk taker, and courageous person. He or she must understand business finance and be able to read financial reports. Executives are Level Three Leaders whose jobs are to forge paths into the future for their companies. We will discuss the levels of leadership in the next chapter.

If you aspire to the executive level, know that the hours are long and the job can be stressful. Your work life will be demanding, and at this level, you must be available at any time of the day or night if a crisis or emergency arises in the company. You must approve all major decisions and actions, and you must be available to other officers and leaders in the company. If you are a parent at the executive level with young children at home, you will most certainly need a support network. You might need to travel for your job or work late with no advance notice. You will need a strong support system for domestic duties and childcare.

Because of the years needed for comprehensive career development and experience, many high-level executives are in their fifties and sixties. By then their children are usually grown, and this is an ideal stage of life to take on more job responsibility because of the greater freedom. Single or childless women also have more freedom to devote time to their careers and might choose to advance to the executive level.

If you are an energetic, competitive lifelong learner and like to be all in, the executive level might be a good choice. The leadership at Level Three is exciting, stimulating, challenging, and ever changing. Heading a company is certainly not easy, but it is rewarding to test your talents, abilities, and years of experience and make a positive impact for your company, customers, and employees. As the head of a company, you will continue to learn because it is a critical component to survive in the competitive work world. You must keep growing personally so you can grow your company. The world is changing every day, and executives must keep pace with the changes to lead their companies into the future. If the description of these challenges interests and excites you, consider executive leadership as an ultimate career goal. Begin planning now to gain the education, skills, and experience you will need to reach the executive level in your career. If you are averse to rapid change and risk, this is probably not the right fit for you.

With this overview, you can begin thinking about what the right job realm and leadership level are for you—now and in the future. Be strategic and intentional about finding your right job and leadership, and you are more likely to enjoy your work and achieve more success throughout your career.

Tips and Takeaways:

- You can be a leader regardless of your title, but higher-level positions carry greater responsibilities.
- A great administrative assistant is able to multitask and problem solve. Managers provide the horsepower to get teams of people moving. CEOs are generally lifelong learners because they must stay current to be successful over long periods of time.
- In all these jobs, people can operate at different levels of leadership. This will be discussed in the next chapter.

CHAPTER 5

THE MIND-SET: THE HIGHER YOU GO, THE MORE YOU GIVE

We all know that if you want to be a great athlete, it takes training. It takes practice. It takes having the right mind-set. Take, for example, a professional golfer. In an article entitled "The Ultimate Mindset for Great Golf," Dr. Bob Winters talks about the level of focus needed to be a winner. He says:

> That is why the most important number in golf is not about par or the comparison scores that others are shooting, but the number one! One shot and one moment is all that you should be thinking about and if you are thinking about the shots from the past or projecting into the future about what you need to shoot, you are not focused into this single moment, which is the present! The idea of being self-full means you are totally immersed into this shot and nothing else. As for the other players, they do not exist. What matters most is what you are doing at this point in time to the exclusion of the world around you. This is what Hall of Fame players such as Hogan, Palmer, Whitworth, Sorenstam and Nicklaus have alluded to when

they said that when they competed they were concentrating so hard on what they were doing it seemed that no one else existed or mattered. They were in a singular, self-full mindset! You should strive to focus your attention and energy into this mindset as well!

If you want to be a great leader, that also takes a certain kind of mind-set. You must first understand this mind-set and then intentionally practice it every day. Just as a professional golfer trains and practices for years, so must a leader train and practice to increase his or her skill level and develop a leadership mind-set.

Most people believe a great leader is brainy, and has lots of talent. That might be true, but we know it takes much more than that. People can be very smart and still not be successful as leaders. In fact, some of the smartest people we know have been miserable failures as leaders. Why? They did not have the mind-set it takes to lead.

So, what is that mind-set?

Believe it or not, it is not very different than the mind-set of the professional golfer. You have to be focused. Focused on what you want to achieve. Focused on what it takes to get there. Focused on you! That is often difficult for women. Dr. Winter calls this level of focus being "self-full."

If you look at your female friends and colleagues, what is it that draws you to them? Generally, they can empathize with you when you explain a situation to them. They are willing to work with you to accomplish a goal in a collaborative manner. They know intuitively what you need. All these things are not coincidences. They are the result of differences in the female brain, and these differences cause women to think and act differently than men. In *Unleash the Power of the Female Brain* by Daniel G.

Amen, he cites many of the special strengths of the female brain. He goes on to say:

Why women may make better bosses:

- Increased empathy
- Collaboration
- Concerned about social cohesion of the group
- Less risk taking behavior
- Greater volume in part of the PFC (executive part of the brain), which is the center of judgment, planning, empathy, and impulse control.

If women possess these attributes, then we need to ask why more women don't get to the top or assertively climb the leadership ladder. We believe it is not about the mind but the mind-set. Let's take a look at each one of the characteristics to see how each can affect leadership for women.

Empathy: Women have the unique ability to put themselves in the situations of others. Because of their social skills and intuitive capabilities, women have an increased understanding of human behavior, relationships, and the struggles that people face in daily life. This ability empowers women to make the workplace more human, which can decrease stress there. However, strength can be a weakness when used in excess. Because women are so good at empathizing, they might also give others passes instead of calling them out for less-than-desirable behaviors. If people aren't held accountable, this strength of empathy can then be interpreted in the workplace as weakness. When women show too much empathy, management might believe they cannot make the tough calls or lead. Remember to balance your empathy and understanding with the appropriate amount of accountability. Raise the bar high, and keep it there for the benefit of your company and its employees. Be compassionate in special or difficult circumstances while simultaneously helping your direct reports excel and keep moving forward. The balance of empathy and accountability is both a skill and art that you can improve with practice.

Collaboration: Women are comfortable working in groups and don't generally hesitate to share power with others. Women might not feel the need to direct every single activity of their groups, and they love to see what ideas, conversation and discussion spark. By being collaborative, they also do not call attention to themselves. Rather, they are focused on the work of the group. This is an excellent leadership strength and helps women to leverage the skills and abilities of everyone on the team. Because many women value collaboration over power, their teams might be more innovative and creative. Women encourage idea sharing and building on ideas. Better overall performance is the result because employees are empowered to be heard and take action.

Because women generally don't seek recognition, this collaboration strength can sometimes work against them. Often, when a woman is the catalyst for great results, she minimizes her contribution. In doing so, she misses the opportunity for company supervisors or executives to understand her strengths and abilities. She might miss out on future opportunities because no one understands her contributions.

Another caution is that when people are strong collaborators, they might try too hard to make things work. Rather than close an unprofitable division, terminate an employee, or stop a research and development project, a collaborative individual might try to find ways to make a situation work. This person might keep persevering when he or she should pursue a different strategy. If you are a person who avoids making tough calls because you want things to work for everyone, then you might not be strategic enough in your thinking. Your inaction can frustrate team members and damage the company's health. Collaboration is certainly a positive skill but must also be used thoughtfully and strategically.

Social Cohesion: You don't need a study to explain this one. Look around. Women tend to be more socially engaged and concerned about the group, while men get down to business and just do the work. Women read both covert and overt messages that help them gauge the reactions and opinions of people—even when there is no dialogue. Women read body language, eye contact, and tone of voice as clues to what groups and individuals are thinking and feeling. They engage socially and respond to the cues they receive. This ability is an advantage for women in the workplace because they can discern negative feedback and messaging that men might miss. They can respond to these messages to create better outcomes for the teams and the companies. However, because socialization is a strength for women, sometimes they can spend too much time socializing. Women can go too deeply into personal conversation when they should be focusing on work. Personal situations and concerns can distract women, and they can forget their professional aims. While concern for others can be a strength, if it causes loss of focus, then it can become a weakness. Be careful to use social skills sparingly and appropriately in the workplace.

Less Risk Taking: Women tend to play it safe. It was not so with Cynthia and Doreen, though, who have learned that calculated risk taking is a necessary part of leadership. Doreen built her company during the recession. This required significant financial investment and risk, and it caused some sleepless nights. Cynthia was able to expand her client list to include global companies during that same recession. As a leader, you must be willing to risk in order to gain reward. Although risks should be thoughtful and calculated, it is still scary when the future is unknown. Many leadership decisions must be made on projections and assumptions about the future, and even the best calculated decisions don't always turn out to be successful. Women business owners must be willing to risk their financial futures to some degree in order to grow personally and for the long-term benefit of the companies. Level Three Leadership requires courageous decisions, both initial and ongoing. As a Level Three Leader, sometimes you will need to take a deep breath and plunge into the unknown. In doing so, you will increase your confidence, courage, and even strategies to cope when things don't work out.

Women can also be less willing to risk relocation than men. With an increasingly global business world, many companies must move individuals around, offer overseas assignments, etc. Men are more likely to pick up and move without hesitation to advance their careers, while women might agonize about leaving their communities—even for a year or two. They might worry it will harm their children or be fearful of leaving friends and family. They might be fearful of the unknown. They might wonder if they will make new friends, like their new communities, or get along with their new coworkers. In reality, travel and relocation benefit children by exposing them to new cultures, people, and ways of living. It helps children become more accepting of different people, and it makes them more resilient too. It also helps women gain confidence by facing fears and trying new things. Think about the big picture and long-term benefits of national and international experiences that broaden a woman's perspective and build her expertise. Don't shrink from tough assignments or new experiences. Embrace them to grow your leadership skills and presence.

Greater volume in the executive part of the female brain can provide better judgment for females because women can process information from multiple sources—without even knowing they are doing it. Because both sides of the female brain interconnect and process information effectively, women might intuitively understand things that men must gather facts and data to understand and quantify. Although this is certainly a strength for women, the ability to see the entire picture can sometimes impair a woman's ability to make snap decisions. Since confident and timely decisions are critical in today's fast-paced business environment women need to be aware of this tendency to hesitate.

In the past, companies did extensive research and planning before making significant changes to product lines, infrastructure, and organizational changes. Today, it is a different world. In the race to be first to market, some planning and judgment have been pushed aside in favor of making the most informed decision in a more timely way. This means that sometimes women must override their need to have all the information before making a judgment and going for it. This makes some women uncomfortable. It often seems risky, as they seek to see and hear all the information to feel more secure in their decisions. The element of risk is always present in business decisions, and women can become better decision-makers as they practice assertiveness in making their decisions.

If you aspire to lead, you might need to alter or change your mind-set to succeed. You must develop the mind-set, but you also must have the energy to lead. It's a bit like carrying a huge load on your shoulders. For some people, leadership is a challenge to see how far they can go. The challenge and responsibility are energizing—even though they are difficult. For other people, leadership feels lonely and heavy, and it wears them out. If the latter is true for you, high-level leadership might not be your best choice.

High-level leadership requires a tremendous amount of energy, and successful leaders embrace the challenge and are fueled by it. If you choose a leadership path, you will certainly have some sleepless nights. Things will go wrong, and you will have to wrestle with problems. However, if you have the mind-set for leadership, you understand that difficulties are part of the package, and you take these challenges in stride. You understand that leadership means putting the welfare of an organization (or community) and its people above yourself. So, honestly assess your own mind-set. Do you have the mind-set and deep desire to lead?

Exercise: Analyze Your Inclination

Pick between the following choices. There are no correct or incorrect answers. The exercise will help you analyze your own values and mind-set for leadership. What is your inclination?

- Join a volleyball team (or workout) or join a work team that will create on a new product
- Watch your favorite reality show or read a work related periodical
- Take a better position on a third shift or stay in your current position with an eight to five job
- Take an educational course on evenings or weekends or have more leisure time
- Move for a huge career opportunity or take a smaller advancement in your current location
- Go to an industry conference or attend a parent's birthday party
- Work for your current supervisor who knows you or move to work for a supervisor who is advancing in your company
- Join a volunteer board where you know other board members but are not invested in the mission or join a board that excites you but you know no one.

Tips and Takeaways:

- If you want to be a great leader, it takes a certain kind of mind-set that is very similar to that of a professional athlete.
- In *Unleash the Power of the Female Brain,* Daniel G. Amen cites many of the special strengths of the female brain, and these strengths can make women better leaders.
- Some of the strengths of the female brain can also be weaknesses if a woman does not have the mind-set to lead.

CHAPTER 6

You Can Have It All...Just Not All at the Same Time

You have probably heard the stories and seen the interviews on television of the woman who seems to have it all. She sits there with every hair in place and perfect makeup and tells you how she manages to work seventy hours a week, be a loving wife and mother, and have time to volunteer for community organizations.

Really?

Many years ago, there was a female television anchor who was held up as the ideal working woman. She had a husband, children, and robust career. She did countless interviews and offered advice about how to find that elusive work-life balance. What most people did not know is she had a nanny, a housecleaner, and a supportive extended family. That is how she could do it all. She had lots of help. The idea of having it all is quite clearly a myth. No one has it all—even if that person has an enjoyable career and a wonderful family. Life is full of compromises and choices. To get one thing, you might have to give up another, and this is certainly true with career choices. Career development is an ongoing juggling act of weighing options and strategically mapping out your course at various stages of your life.

In today's demanding world, you can be a leader and have it all—just not all at the same time. We live in a world where we are used to being able to get what we need instantly. However, when it comes to your career, it is more complex than that and requires thoughtful planning. It also takes years to develop your skills and expertise. No one gets there instantly. It takes years to create a proven track record of success. It takes years to develop the experience and maturity needed to be a Level Three Leader. So, planning your career development should be seen as a lifetime journey with many twists and turns.

Talent is certainly an essential element to success, but it is only one of the necessary ingredients. The truth is that most successful people have been at their crafts for many years. For example, many people assumed Tiger Woods was an overnight success, but he started playing golf at the age of three. Taylor Swift became interested in music at the age of nine. Meryl Streep, whom many consider the most successful actress of all time, began acting in high school plays. All have devoted countless hours to perfecting their crafts. It might appear to some they were overnight sensations, but that is simply not true. Very few really become an overnight success. Successful people study and practice their crafts for years before they make splashes that others notice. Even after people attain success in their fields, they still don't have it all. They are required to give some things up for other things that are important to them, and you will too.

So, what do you need to do to have it all at some point?

Stay in the Game. You Can't Drop Out.

No one becomes a leader overnight. It takes time and consistent dedication throughout a lifetime. Women who want to build successful careers and become leaders should understand something important. Even if they can't go full force in their current life stages, they should not drop out. Why? It is pretty simple. Their peers and competitors are moving forward. Employers won't wait around for women who have dropped out to come back. Companies will replace you with a man or woman who stayed in the game to build his or her career. The sad reality is that when women drop out of work and career development, even for five or ten years, and then want to return to the working world, they find themselves unable to get jobs at the levels they left. Sometimes they can't even get jobs at all—at any level.

When a woman drops out of her field, she is not gaining the experiences needed to stay current and become an expert in that field. Think of how quickly the world is changing. The skills that were critical to many jobs even a few short years ago are no longer valued. When women opt out, they might need to go through a re-education process and build new skills to return to the workplace. In contrast, women who have stayed current will cost employers less time and money in training, be productive much faster, and provide better returns for their companies.

Another advantage to staying in the working world is the important relationships you build...or lose when you quit. Our networks and contacts are critical to our successes. The old saying is true—it's not what you know; it's who you know. In other words, relationships with people who know our abilities and are invested in our successes can help us gain referrals and promotions. People like to do business with people they know and trust. When women drop out and lose their business contacts, they might end up out of touch and going it alone when they attempt to reenter the business world. This makes it much harder to get ahead.

Research shows that when women drop out of work for a period of time, they compromise their lifelong earning potential.

They never catch up to the incomes of peers who stayed in the working world. In addition to lost income for the period of time when a woman doesn't work, she reenters the job market at a much lower pay rate. Employers will use her dropping out to their financial benefit. It will take years to regain the previous income, and many never recoup their pay positions or reach their previous earning potential.

Another difficulty for women who drop out of work is that many employers believe they are less motivated and not ambitious enough. They might think these women don't have the drive and commitment needed in potential leaders. It also calls into question a woman's ability to problem solve and strategize. If a woman could not figure out how to continue to work and balance her life, how could she possibly be strategic for the company?

Finally, women who drop out are dependent on others for their financial security. Even those who are in wonderful relationships with their partners or spouses are in vulnerable positions. What if the relationship dissolves in the future? What if your partner is injured or killed? How will you manage? From an employer's perspective, it is hard to trust in the leadership ability of someone who has placed himself or herself in a dependent position.

For men, dropping out has not traditionally been an option. In contrast, women have been given passes to drop out of work and be dependent if they have partners or spouses who could support them. Consider the resiliency and strength of men. They problem solve how to work around frustrations and stay in the game because they must.

Before you drop out, consider the big picture and possible consequences over your lifetime. Think strategically beyond this particular stage of your life to determine your long-term goals. Be intentional about how to achieve them. This is where a life or business coach might be helpful. (There will be more about that in chapter twenty.)

Be Strategic about Your Career over a Lifetime

Your career is like a journey. To reach your destination, you must have an end goal established. After that, you can develop a road map to take you there. Your final destination might change over time, but you can always make adjustments or build a new route. If you don't know where you are going, though, you will likely become lost. You could end up somewhere you never wanted to be. Planning your lifetime career journey is much the same process as planning a road trip. The following are some tips to consider.

If your goal is to someday lead an organization, start by doing some research into the future position you are interested in. What hard and soft skills will you need to move forward?

- What positions will you need to hold to build your résumé and experience?
- Will you need to work in a variety of different roles within the company to be considered for a promotion?
- Is the road to your goal through the finance area or engineering or sales?
- Will you need to lead projects or teams?
- Are there certain degrees or certifications that must be obtained?
- What competencies will you need to demonstrate?
- If you serve on a board or do volunteer work, is that considered a valuable experience?

Once you have developed this road map or list, you should regularly check to see if you are on the right path because the business world is constantly changing. Be intentional about everything you do. A successful career does not happen by accident. It takes time and effort to build a résumé and contacts.

You must also think strategically about the timing of your career development. Do you want to be at the top of your game in your thirties? Maybe not. If you are trying to juggle a home life that includes children, you might want to use your thirties as a time to strategically build your résumé by working part time, gaining important certifications and trainings, and making contributions to your field. Later, as your children become more independent, you can accelerate your progress and build on the foundation you've created. If you plan to fast-track your career and family at the same time, be sure you have excellent support systems in place for childcare and domestic chores.

No matter what your personal situation, you will need to advocate for yourself to build your career. Society is not changing very rapidly in how it views female leaders—even though a recent study said that by the year 2040 the majority of corporate CEOs will be women. In the meantime, don't wait for things to change. Make them change for your future by finding and pursuing opportunities. Remember, it can take as many as twenty years to be an expert in your field, so plan your career development with this reality in mind.

Make Adjustments to Your Plan

History has shown that many things can stall a career journey or require you to create a completely new road map.

- Your company goes through downsizing.
- There is a change of ownership that shakes up management and eliminates positions.
- The company you work for closes its doors.
- You decide you need to make a change or try a different industry, geographic area, or corporate culture.
- You want to leave the corporate world altogether and start your own business.

We all know we have to make adjustments and remain flexible because nothing ever goes completely as planned. There is no such thing as a road map that endures for a lifetime. If you choose the corporate path, you might find yourself jumping from lily pad to lily pad trying to advance. Sometimes the stops are brief. You learn what you need to know and move to the next level when it is time. Maybe you find that the job is not the right fit, and you hop to another company or position. At each stop, you must be sure that the next destination is moving you closer to the goal.

If you decide to leave the corporate world and go into business for yourself, you must be a risk taker and willing to live with the uncertainty that is part of owning a business. The statistics say it all. According to the Small Business Administration, "about half of all new establishments survive five years or more and about one-third survive 10 years or more." Still, every year people open new businesses. The adjustments you will need to make here are huge—especially if you have come from the corporate world. You will have fewer resources, work more hours, and wear more hats.

Whether you go the corporate route or start your own business you will need to make many adjustments throughout your business journey.

Pace Yourself

You might have heard the saying that it is not a sprint but a marathon. That is exactly how you must view your career planning over your lifetime. The truth is that very few people will ever be CEOs of significant enterprises in their twenties. Some might be CEOs in their thirties, but that is also rare. It's important to pace yourself and be realistic about how quickly you want to move up the ladder. Move too slowly and you can stagnate. Move too fast and you might burn yourself out. Here are a few things to consider as you choose your rate of growth.

Much has been written about the work-life balance. We won't even attempt to tackle that here. What we do suggest is having some kind of life outside of work. For every person, the amount of time outside work that is needed to be happy is different. The activities that bring you happiness are also different. The trick is to understand how your pace of work affects your ability to do the things you love.

If you are a high-powered worker, you might opt out of a lot of extracurricular activities. You might charge ahead and love tackling a big project at work that keeps you working long past when others have called it quits for the day. If you are this type of person and have a family, you will need their support to reach your career goals. You will need family members to help around the house with cooking and cleaning. You are not neglectful of your family just because you are not available to wait on them twenty-four/seven. You should not feel guilty. In fact, research shows that kids who must help around the house are more self-confident and independent and have more positive self-images. The truth is no one can do it all, so don't even try to work long hours and be supermom. You must have systems and support in place...or slow down your pace. If you don't make some adjustments, both you and your family will suffer and become resentful. If the pace is too overwhelming, you might consider slowing down a bit until the children are older and can be more independent.

Pace is necessary to avoid burning out. If you go all out too soon, you might not have the energy (or perhaps health) to have a long and successful career. Everyone knows people at the height of their careers who just couldn't take it anymore and chose to step back or step out of corporate life. They were tired, out of ideas, and burned out. They just wanted simpler lives.

If you think about it, most people are now working much longer than ever before. Your career might span more than fifty years, and if you don't pace yourself, you simply won't last.

Finally, think about your personal tolerance for stress. Every person is different in what stresses them. Stress is sometimes OK. In fact, it can be motivating. You should aim to move at a pace where you can manage the stress and let it fuel your success—not sabotage it.

So, what is the bottom line?

Yes, you can have it all! You can have both a great career and a wonderful, rich personal life. Understand, though, you will need to make intentional choices because you probably can't have it all at the same time.

Tips and Takeaways:

- To have a long and successful career, you must understand that career development is an ongoing juggling act of weighing options and strategically mapping out your course at various stages of your life.
- Women who drop out of the workplace run the risk of losing their networks and falling behind on critical skills.
- While many appear to be overnight successes, the truth is it can take as many as twenty years to become an expert in your field.

PART 2: DO YOU HAVE WHAT IT TAKES?

CHAPTER 7

ELEVEN TRAITS OF TRUE LEADERS

L eadership is a lifelong journey of learning and growth. Great leaders share common traits that make them outstanding, and in this chapter we will present these traits and describe specifically what behaviors exemplify them. Understand that since leadership is a process of development, you will need to learn and practice these traits until they become part of your tool kit and are integrated into your way of being and thinking. Some of the traits are innate gifts. This means you might have more limited potential in some areas compared to someone else who possesses this innate gift. Don't be discouraged, however. Life isn't perfect, and people aren't either. Just keep developing your leadership traits—no matter what your own gifts happen to be. You will become a better person and a better leader in the process. People can't predict their ultimate potential until they put themselves to the test. You will certainly fail many times in your journey. However, if you are energized and excited about leadership and if you understand the sacrifices and embrace them, then you will stay focused on your growth and opportunities. Don't let obstacles throw you off track. Now, let's look at the amazing traits of great leaders.

Passionate

> There is no greatness without a passion to be
> great, whether it's the aspiration of an athlete or
> an artist, a scientist, a parent, or a businessperson.
> — *ANTHONY ROBBINS*

What does the dictionary say about the word "passionate"? Here are some definitions to consider from *Webster's Dictionary*: "1. Capable of, affected by, or having intense feeling; 2. Enthusiastic, ardent; 3. Easily aroused to anger."

Anger?

Think about that. We don't get angry unless we care about things, do we? Apathetic people don't usually get very angry. Passion is the antithesis of apathy. Consider some of the words the thesaurus equates to "passionate": aroused, afire, heated, intense, stimulated, activated, zealous, energized, vibrant, fervent, and spirited. Do you get the idea? This describes an energetic, engaged, and active person. A person who makes things happen. A leader.

Level Three Leaders need fire in their bellies. Without this passion, high-level success is difficult—if not impossible. Passion fuels the fire needed to run faster and jump higher. It produces the adrenaline needed to think sharper, last longer, and move quickly. Passion steels our resolve to face fear, discouragement, opposition, defeat, loneliness, and criticism and still keep going. It empowers us to be superhuman with the strength of Hercules when needed.

Without passion, people who aspire to high-level leadership will never make it. They will run out of gas before the finish line, and other competitors will leave them in the dust.

Certainly, you can lead at some levels and in many ways without a high level of passion. However, Level Three Leaders need to be all in, and only passion will give people the energy to keep going over time.

We should clarify that passion does not need to be loud, boisterous, obnoxious, or in your face. Passion is an inner feeling that drives you. You feel this when something matters so strongly that you cannot deny it. You can't run away from it, and you don't want to. You are resolved to do this thing that calls you. There are certainly as many objects of human passion as there are stars in the sky. The depth of your own passion for something will dictate how much energy and time you are willing to devote to the cause.

As you evaluate the level at which you want to serve, think about how much passion you have for this thing. Do you care enough to weather the inevitable storms on the journey? We advise potential leaders to quantify the cost of success and choose the right level for your passion. Leading with passion energizes you and the people you lead, and it is a necessary ingredient for all great leaders.

Responsible

> The person who complains about the way the ball
> bounces is likely to be the one who dropped it.
> —*Lou Holtz*

It's interesting that the most notable quotes on responsibility are all by men. Does that mean men are more willing to carry the burden of responsibility? Or, is it that women are programmed to take passes? Many women are programmed from an early age to defer to men. Before we examine this closely, though, let's look at what responsibility is. The classic *Webster's Dictionary* definition of responsible is: "1. having the job or duty of dealing with or taking care of something or someone; 2. able to be trusted to do what is right or to do the things that is expected or required; 3. involving important duties, decisions, etc., that you are trusted to do." What does that have to do with leadership? Everything.

There is only one way to reach for another rung as you climb the ladder of success toward becoming a leader. It is to take on more responsibility. More responsibility means caring for more people; expanding the scope of your duties; broadening your reach; becoming more involved, visible, and vocal; taking on more risk; and entering the realm where stakes are higher. Being responsible necessitates that every day your focus is on the company, its people, its customers, its principles, its image, its profits, and its security—*not* on yourself.

Respected leaders stand in the back of the team for praise and in front of the team for criticism. In taking responsibility, they earn the trust of their teams, peers, and customers.

Responsible people do not blame others. George Washington Carver said, "Ninety-nine percent of all failures come from people who have a habit of making excuses." Why? Because taking personal responsibility is the only way people grow. We are in control of what we think, how we feel, the actions we take, and the reactions we choose. Responsible people understand this basic principle and work to improve and solve problems when things go wrong instead of placing blame.

If you find yourself blaming others, even if it's only in your inner thoughts or attitude, you've got some work to do if you aspire to be a leader. Your current blaming attitude will show up in all kinds of subtle ways: resentment, gossip, avoidance, denial, resistance, and procrastination. It will show up in your facial expression, body language, voice inflection, and eye contact—even if you never say a word about it. Who wants to spend time with or promote someone with those characteristics? The only way for you to move forward toward success and leadership is to grow up and take responsibility. No excuses!

Resilient

> If there's nobody in your way, it's because
> you're not going anywhere.
> —*Robert F. Kennedy*

Webster's Dictionary defines "resiliency" as "the act of rebounding." The dictionary defines "rebound" as "to spring or bound back." Think of a ball thrown to the floor. It doesn't stay there, does it? A ball thrown to the floor bounces higher than it started. Leaders bounce back. They don't just *come* back. When leaders face roadblocks, hit walls, fall flat on their faces, or encounter any number of other setbacks, they bound back. They aim higher and jump higher than before and with greater resolve.

High-level leaders possess resiliency and the unique ability to focus on missions and visions instead of themselves. This outward vision is so strong that nothing can deter them. Not criticism, not fear, and not any of the obstacles that would discourage many others. Passion and the resolve to serve their families, companies, and people drive true leaders. This passion empowers them to stay single minded in their quests to march toward their stated goals. They are not squeamish about facing whatever comes. Passion fuels their fire and solidifies their purpose and determination.

"This is what leadership is all about: staking your ground ahead of where opinion is, not simply following the popular opinion of the moment" (Doris Kearns Goodwin). Great leaders are tenacious and tough with the will to carry on and inspire others to do the same. A leader's task is to get people from where they are to where they have not been. They need to be fearless in leading these charges. A leader must possess not only the will, but the capacity to demonstrate resiliency in such a way that it inspires confidence in others to follow.

We like the words *Roget's Thesaurus* associates with resiliency: buoyant, elastic, hardy, irrepressible, quick to recover, rebounding, snapping back, strong, supple, and tough. Read those words and think about them. They describe a person with great inner strength and reserves. Those character qualities are necessary for leadership at the highest levels.

Focused

> To focus means to bring your attention to
> the center, to concentrate on one thing
> intently in order to gain clarity.
> — *CHERYL RICHARDSON*

Just what is focus, and why is it critical to success in leadership? Focus is the ability to keep your center of attention on the most important goal for as long as it takes to get the results you need. It means making the goal your top priority. It means concentrating on it, dedicating time to it, revolving around it, and making it the center of your world. Great leaders focus until they are able to see clearly. They focus to filter out distractions and negative messages. They focus to look past the symptoms and get to the problems' cores in order to find solutions.

The Level Three Leadership focus is not within everyone's capacity. Nearly all of us can focus on a given task for a finite period of time. Most people can stay focused a little longer when something is really important to them or when the environment around them is quiet and calm. The ability to stay focused in the midst of chaos is rare. Great leaders can filter through noise, dissent, frustration, discouragement, fear, threat, and complexity to produce results. These leaders see past the distractions that pull others off track. They drill down to simplify and clarify solutions. They are effective in a noisy world because they can quiet their own brains and thoughts. They create inner calm in the midst of a storm so they can think and lead.

Observe a great leader during crisis, and you will see someone who is thinking, creating solutions, directing activities, and affecting outcomes. High-level leaders not only focus, but can discern what to focus on. When others are in despair or feel confused, a great leader is solving problems and implementing solutions. The ability to focus empowers a great leader to be effective.

It is important to note that the ability to laser focus can sometimes appear like not paying attention. For example, in a highly interactive meeting, a Level Three Leader might appear far away. He or she might be quietly reflecting while others are animated and engaged. Don't be fooled. This leader is highly engaged in selective thinking and concentration. He or she is putting pieces of the puzzle together by capturing new insights and information gleaned during the meeting. The leader might not be ready to offer his or her thoughts yet, but rest assured that he or she is actively thinking. Often, this focused thought can only be facilitated by filtering out stimuli that would distract from the process. Profound solutions are in the making!

Certainly, the ability to focus can be developed just like any skill. This requires intentional effort and perseverance—even to the point where it might feel as if your brain hurts. However, there is no question that advancing your leadership means improving your ability to focus on what's important. When things are chaotic and others look to you for leadership, focus will empower you to clarify the issues and find solutions. Focus will enable you to simplify complex situations. "Simplicity is ultimately a matter of focus" (Ann Voskamp).

Visionary

> The very essence of leadership is [that] you have
> a vision. It's got to be a vision you articulate
> clearly and forcefully on every occasion.
> —*THEODORE HESBURGH*

> Vision is the art of seeing the invisible.
> —*JONATHAN SWIFT*

What are we talking about when we say "vision"? Vision takes things to a whole new level. Here are some definitions of "visionary" to clarify our concept: "1. Thinking about or planning the future with imagination or wisdom; 2. A person with original ideas about what the future will or could be like."

Just why is vision important to leadership? Simply put, vision inspires. It inspires because vision helps people see a brighter, better future. Vision challenges people to see things differently, and it excites them with new possibilities. Visionary leaders are imaginative, creative, inventive, ingenious, enterprising, and innovative. These qualities inspire others not only to follow a visionary leader, but also to give their best to the team, company, and effort. Visionary leaders are very different (and infinitely more effective) than the old "command and control" bosses of the past. Bossing people around rarely inspires them to give their very best. Rather, bossing provokes resistance and resentment. In contrast, visionary leaders are like the pioneers who blazed new trails into the wilderness and created new opportunities for their families and communities.

What many people do not understand is that vision doesn't materialize from nowhere or out of the clear blue sky. Visionary leaders are constantly searching for and tracking sources of information and inspiration to develop their farsighted visions. Visionary leaders are usually voracious readers of books, periodicals, quotes, signs, blogs, and anything else they can get their eyes on. Visionary leaders are listeners. They understand they will learn much more by listening, and so they do. They listen to the news, public chatter, family and friends, coworkers, fellow board members or meeting participants, and noises and sounds. Visionary leaders listen for clues and puzzle pieces to connect the dots into the future. These leaders are curious, and they are thinkers. They watch people and learn. Visionary leaders track and consider cultural shifts, current trends and needs, and the economic climate. They consider how these will affect people now and in the future. The constant, unstoppable intellectual activity of a visionary leader empowers him or her to see and create the future.

A visionary might appear calm and quiet on the surface, but know that he or she is engaged in constant intellectual activity under that quiet exterior. A visionary maintains consistent energy and activity that is often not discernible to anyone else. However, it becomes evident when the leader is ready to share the vision. These creative and visionary gifts are exceptional ones that not everyone possesses. However, vision is a powerful positive force in mobilizing companies and people to achieve seemingly impossible futures.

Inspiring

> If your actions inspire others to dream more, learn more, do more and become more, you are a leader.
> —JOHN QUINCY ADAMS

Inspiration is a necessary quality of leadership because it motivates people to take action and get things done. A leader might have lots of great ideas, but if he or she can't inspire the team or company, it's difficult to succeed. More clearly defined, to "inspire" is: "1. to fill with an animating, quickening, or exalting influence; 2. to produce or arouse (a feeling, thought, etc.); 3. to influence or impel."

There is something compelling and electrifying about a leader who is truly inspirational. An inspirational leader expands the vision of the company and creates excitement and longing for more. He or she broadens people's perspectives and stimulates their emotions. An inspirational leader provokes others and influences them to raise the bar and work harder to make the future vision a reality.

Now we have an idea of what inspirational leaders do, but just how do these leaders do it? Why do they do it, and what is the fuel for their fire? In short, an inspirational leader is unequivocally passionate about the mission and vision of their company. This passion is heartfelt, genuine, and palpable. A truly inspirational leader would nearly lay down his or her life in the pursuit of this thing he or she believes so deeply in. The level of passion is moving. It is emotional. It generates a positive energy that people want to be around and be part of. You should understand that inspirational leadership is not frivolous or haphazard. It is a passion that comes from deep thought, careful planning and love for the organization and its mission, people, and customers. True passion has an uplifting and stimulating authenticity. Inspirational leadership is also regenerating—particularly to an organization that has gone stale and lost its way. Inspirational leadership awakens the senses and feeds the weary soul. It is liberating because it imparts a sense of purpose that drives people and teams forward.

Make no mistake—the most successful organizations possess inspirational leaders at many levels. These leaders are the lifeblood of the organization and the engines that drive the organization forward. Inspirational leaders don't need titles to elevate their missions and motivate others. They do it because of who they are and what they believe. Their messages are compelling because they have integrity.

So, ask yourself what you're genuinely passionate about and how you're using your passion to inspire others. What unique insights can you share to influence positive outcomes? Are you an active, positive force or a passive, inactive observer? Awaken your own passions and you can begin to inspire others!

Discerning

> Some people think they have discernment
> when actually they are just suspicious.
> Suspicion comes out of the unrenewed mind;
> discernment comes out of the renewed spirit.
> —*Joyce Meyer*

What do we mean by "discernment"? *Webster's Dictionary* says "discernment" is: "1. showing insight and understanding; 2. showing good or outstanding judgment; 3. to perceive by the sight or some other sense or by the intellect; 4. to distinguish mentally; recognize as distinct or different; discriminate."

A discerning person is wise, insightful, perceptive, and prudent. Discernment might seem like an elusive quality for a leader, but discernment is at the heart of wisdom, and every leader needs to be wise. So, how does one acquire wisdom and insight? How does a leader become discerning, and why is it important?

Leaders use discernment every day in all kinds of circumstances. For example, a CEO must discern what strategies and initiatives to invest in for the company's success and which ones are not worthy to pursue. A board member must discern between perceived threats and real threats to the company's future. Leaders at all levels must discern between truth and fiction in marketing, communication, vendor relationships, and office politics. Executives must discern changes in popular culture, economic climate, and the real and perceived needs of customers. They must discern how that all affects the company, its products and services, and its future strategies.

Leaders do not become wise and discerning by simply wishing for it. Insight is the result of many years of hard work and experience, and there is no substitute for putting in your time to achieve this admirable quality. In the book *Talent Is Overrated,* author Geoff Colvin makes the point that it takes an average of twenty years of intentional work to become an expert in your field. You must build a vast knowledge base to be an expert, and this obviously takes time and effort. To complicate things, a leader must be an expert on all kinds of subjects. First, a leader becomes an expert in his or her industry, but that alone is not enough. An executive must also be knowledgeable in finance, human-resources issues, marketing, legal concerns, global industry, business operations, communication, IT, and a host of other areas. In other words, a great leader must have the "right stuff." His or her acquired knowledge will empower that leader with insights that others who are less experienced would miss. That leader's vast knowledge base enables him or her to be discerning in the hundreds of small and large decisions faced every day and to tie everything into the company's larger goals and direction.

A discerning leader has not merely built a solid foundation of vast knowledge and understanding, but continues to add new and current information to this store of knowledge. A great leader is a lifelong learner and is constantly engaged in the acquisition of new information. He or she listens, watches, reads, and questions as part of his or her daily lifestyle. For example, Doreen reads multiple books, periodicals, articles, and blogs simultaneously while listening to relevant radio broadcasts, Internet videos and broadcasts, and television broadcasts. She is constantly seeking new and current information in her industry; finance; marketing; general business and operations; culture; and local, national, and global trends.

Level Three Leaders also engage in conversations on the topics we've described above. This challenges their perspectives and enhances the application of their knowledge. We can tell you that high-level executives are usually *not* sitting on sofas and watching television and movies for pure entertainment! Level Three Leaders have earned their positions by years of work and that has empowered them with discernment to lead their companies and people on prudent pathways to successful outcomes. If you aspire to be a Level Three Leader, make time to earn your unofficial degree in discernment.

Humble

> You have a good many little gifts and virtues, but
> there is no need of parading them, for conceit
> spoils the finest genius. There is not much danger
> that real talent or goodness will be overlooked long,
> and the greatest charm of all powers is modesty.
> —*Louisa May Alcott*

> Pride is concerned with who is right.
> Humility is concerned with what is right.
> —*Ezra Taft Benson*

> Nobody stands taller than those
> willing to stand corrected.
> — *William Safire*

Truly great leaders possess humility. Great leaders are humble not because they ought to be, but because of how they genuinely see the world and their place in it. The dictionary describes a humble person as: "1. not proud or arrogant; modest; 2. low in rank, importance, status; 3. courteously respectful." Here are synonyms that describe those who are humble: unpretending, unpretentious, submissive, unassuming, and polite. Think about those qualities. Most people are comfortable around a humble person. People usually feel accepted and heard when with someone humble. People don't feel as if they need to compete with a humble person, and they usually feel calm rather than stressed in a humble person's presence.

In contrast, look at the antonyms for the word "humble": proud, exalted, rude, insolent, elevate, and exalt. These words are stark contrasts. Doreen gets worked up just reading the antonyms! Nobody wants to be with someone who is proud, rude, or insolent—and people sure don't want to be subject to a leader with those qualities!

What is going on with humble leaders? Why are they that way? It is not because they think less of themselves. It is because they think more of others. Humble leaders are confident and competent. They are humble because they focus on getting the job done. They focus on the mission and vision, the best interest of the company and its people, customers, strategy, and a host of other things rather than themselves. Humble, effective leaders are not thinking about how to enhance their images or gain recognition. These are simply not the most important things to them. That is what is attractive about humble people. Being humble is an authentic way of being. Fortunately, it is a character quality people can choose to cultivate. It comes from the inner being and must be cultivated in the heart and soul. Being humble is seeing oneself with a balanced perspective rather than an elevated one. It is choosing to go last instead of pushing to be first. It is standing in front of team members for criticism and in the back for praise. It is a willingness to be wrong and being gracious in the process. It is genuinely valuing the contributions of others instead of needing to talk about one's own. It is listening to (and acknowledging) another point of view instead of interrupting to interject one's own. It is seeking help instead of pretending to know it all.

Humble leaders genuinely congratulate others when they are recognized rather than needing to boast about their own accomplishments. Team members will go above and beyond for a truly humble leader because that leader is giving his or her best to and for the team. However, when a leader is arrogant, rude, or prideful, subordinates might grudgingly comply with the leader's orders by doing only what is required of them.

Take a hard look at yourself. What would others say about you—humble or proud? Start exercising and strengthening your "humble muscle" to become a leader others *want* to follow.

Courageous

> Courage is the virtue that makes possible all
> the other virtues common to exceptional
> leaders: honesty, integrity, confidence,
> compassion, and humility. In short, leaders
> who lack courage aren't leaders.
> —*FAST COMPANY, 2004*

> You gain strength, courage, and confidence
> by every experience in which you really stop
> to look fear in the face. You must do the
> thing which you think you cannot do.
> —*ELEANOR ROOSEVELT*

Leaders need courage, and the higher your level of leadership, the more courage you need. The good news is that developing courage is like developing a muscle. The more you exercise it, the stronger it becomes. Believe us—you will need strong courage as a high-level leader! Leaders exercise courage just about every day. This includes courage to:

- Speak and hear the truth.
- Stand up for what they know is right.
- Pursue audacious goals.
- Take blame.
- Empower and trust others.

- Focus on the big picture when everyone else is fixated on the next quarter.
- Fail.
- Know when to quit.
- Forge a path when there isn't one.

Great courage is the cornerstone of great leadership, and this trait is often the most challenging for women. From childhood, girls are taught to be nice, quiet, and non-confrontational. They're told to follow directions, be perfect, and play it safe. However, none of these qualities fosters the courage women need for high-level leadership. We cheat girls out of reaching their potential when we fail to develop their courage. This is perhaps the most important thing everyone can do to promote leadership for women—challenge them.

If you personally aspire to lead well, focus on developing your courage. Take risks. Face physical and mental challenges. Place yourself in situations that scare you, and seek the support and training necessary to succeed.

When Doreen's youngest daughter, Paige, was growing up, she was naturally timid. Paige was cautious and wanted to know all the details to feel safe before agreeing to a new experience. Being the adventurous and risk-taking mom Doreen was, she pushed Paige constantly. Yes, she felt stressed by it. Yes, she whined, cried, resisted, and complained. Doreen, though, never let Paige off the hook. Doreen encouraged and challenged Paige to test her limits. Doreen pushed her to risk failure and required that she forge ahead in the face of uncertainty. It was a constant battle, and Doreen often worried Paige would end up in therapy as an adult to seek comfort and solace from her stressful past. Doreen is happy to report the opposite happened. Today, Paige is a confident woman who leads fearlessly and is promoted to leadership roles wherever she works or volunteers. She embraces physical challenges and adventure. She is also raising her own fearless daughters! Paige understands the importance of teaching her girls to be courageous and is fully invested in the process along with her girls' dad, Jake.

Challenging girls and women to be strong is critical to building their leadership potential. The good news is it's never too late. If your own "courage muscle" needs development, start moving outside your comfort zone. Don't let the sensation of fear convince you that you are too weak to have courage. Seek opportunities that provoke some fear. Learn to "do the thing you think you cannot do" (Eleanor Roosevelt). Find coaches and mentors who will challenge you to be more than you imagine. We are all capable of much more than we think, and sometimes we need someone else to encourage and push us to that new place. Courage is the essential foundation of leadership, and Nike's tag line applies to developing courage: just do it!

Understanding

> We make a living by what we get. We make a life by what we give.
> —*WINSTON CHURCHILL*

> A life spent centering only on itself will in the end occupy a very, very small universe.
> —*JOHN GLENN*

> As much as we need a prosperous economy, we also need prosperity of kindness and decency.
> —*CAROLINE KENNEDY SCHLOSSBERG*

It is important to define the "understanding" we believe is necessary at all levels of leadership. It is not necessarily understanding things (although, that's important too); we believe it is more important for every great leader to understand people. Here is how the dictionary defines "understanding": "1. the ability to understand something; comprehension; 2. sympathetically aware of other people's feelings; tolerant and forgiving; 3. having insight or good judgment."

There are many things a leader needs to understand on many levels. Of course, leaders need to understand their industries, leadership, and a host of other things we discuss in this book. What we'd like to cover here is the understanding of people—understanding how to be compassionate and still get the job done. How do leaders balance understanding with the goals of the workplace?

Female leaders have some unique advantages when it comes to understanding. When women learn how to use their gifts wisely, it makes a very positive impact in the workplace. Women are intuitive. They process information and understand the people around them without consciously trying. Women are detail oriented. They notice body language, facial expressions, voice inflection, and eye contact, and they intuitively derive meaning from this information. This helps them understand people. In contrast, male leaders are sometimes clueless about the subtle nuances of social interactions around them. Men might not appreciate that subtle social cues are critical to understanding the impact of culture, policies, initiatives, and team dynamics on productivity and morale. As a result, morale might deteriorate, and a company could lose key people before the leader even realizes there is a problem.

As an example of understanding leadership, Doreen worked in a company when an employee's home burned down. Her family lost everything. The empathetic and compassionate female leader organized a "shower" for fellow employees to provide basic items to the family as they moved into temporary housing after the fire. This act of kindness boosted team spirit, morale, and the sense of community within the company. It also enabled the employee to return to work sooner and more productively since she did not need to worry about basic needs for her family.

Understand that a leader who is unaware or personally unengaged can create an I-don't-care attitude among team members. It is difficult for employees to follow someone and give their best to a leader who doesn't believe in or give his or her best to team members. In contrast, employees who feel cared for by their leaders go above and beyond the required work to give their very best to the company. This is a gift. Giving one's best is a gift offered only to worthy causes or people that one believes in. As a leader, be intentional about caring for your people and being worthy of their best.

We have one word of caution on this subject for female leaders. It is important for leaders to understand how to care for others and also understand the boundaries of over-caring. Business life is different than personal life, and effective leaders understand how to care but balance that caring with company policies. They work according to the company's best interest. It is inappropriate to compromise company integrity or policies out of emotion for an employee who is having a difficult time. Doing so can foster resentment in other employees and compromise team morale. Appropriate care for employees is an art—not a science—and great leaders understand how to balance business with personal needs of employees.

Quick Thinking

If everyone is thinking alike, then
somebody isn't thinking.
—*George Patton*

If you're not faster than your competitor,
you're in a tenuous position, and if you're
only half as fast, you're terminal.
— *George Salk*

Even if you're on the right track, you'll
get run over if you just sit there.
— *Will Rogers*

To be clear about what we mean by "quick thinking," let's look at what the dictionary says about each word. "Quick" indicates "moving fast or doing something in a short time" and also "prompt to understand, think, or learn; intelligent." Thinking is "a way of reasoning; judgment." So, what we mean by "quick thinking" is that a leader has the intelligence to quickly understand and judge situations and the ability to move fast to make adjustments in a short time.

For successful leaders, quick thinking is an essential trait. Level Three Leaders must constantly assess the current business environment, and that includes competition, market fluctuations, cultural shifts, financial parameters, company resources and capabilities, and a host of other indicators. A Level Three Leader must monitor internal and external fluctuations, but this leader must also possess the intellect, creativity, experience, knowledge, and courage to adjust quickly enough to keep the company a formidable competitor in the business world. This is not for the faint of heart! In assessing your own desire for Level Three Leadership, think not only about your intellectual agility, but also about your courage and willingness to bear the stress and pressure of the quick thinking required of you every day as an executive, CEO, or president.

Even if you decide Level Three Leadership is not for you, quick thinking is still required to some degree at all levels of leadership. Whenever you bear responsibility for the outcome of something, you are called on for quick thinking—especially in emergencies or crisis situations. When a crisis happens, you must think and solve the problem quickly because people are depending on you. It is crucial to maintain a clear head, to focus, to set emotion and fear aside, quickly sort the available information, and reach a solution. If you typically fall apart in a crisis situation or are not able to think clearly, we recommend you work on improving your quick thinking before you aspire to a leadership position.

We have all seen people in a crisis who wring their hands and look desperately around for someone to take action. Although these can be good and caring people, they are not leaders. Hesitation and anxiety are the observable traits of a follower. We will also risk saying that some leadership traits we've listed can be flexible as you develop your leadership skills, but this is not one of them. Quick thinking is a necessary trait for leaders to be respected and for others to choose to follow them. Remember, you are only a leader if people willingly choose to follow you. Leadership is not anointed by title. It is earned by character, and quick thinking is one of the essential traits.

Exercise: Rate Yourself

Rate yourself from 1 to 10 on each of the leadership traits. One represents very little skill or experience with the trait, five would be average and ten means that you excel at exhibiting this trait. Take the trait with the lowest score and craft a development plan to improve. Here are some possible options:

- Do online research to find articles and suggestions for personal growth. Practice and apply what you learn on a daily basis.
- Find a book on that specific topic by a noted authority. One example is *The Leadership Challenge: How to Make Extraordinary Things Happen in Organizations* by James M. Kouzes and Barry Posner.
- Attend a seminar or conference. Many local chambers offer programs for leadership development.
- Take an online course or university course in leadership.

- Find a mentor or hire a coach (more about that in Chapter 20)
- Observe leaders you admire and analyze how they use their skills. Ask them to talk to you about how they employ these traits in their daily lives.

Tips and Takeaways:

- Leaders possess some specific traits that are evident at every level of leadership.
- Developing leadership traits requires intentional practice.
- Assess your own strength in leadership traits, and develop areas where you are weak.

CHAPTER 8

THE ART OF BALANCING LEADERSHIP TRAITS

I n the 2002 *Ivey Business Journal,* Stephen Bernhut said in "Primal Leadership with Daniel Goleman" that, "Leadership is the art of getting work done through other people."

Leadership truly is an art that is achieved through balancing leadership traits. Now that you understand what we believe to be the character traits of great leaders, it's important to know that developing these traits is a lifelong journey. At different points in your career or in certain roles different traits can be more important.

For example, imagine your company is in a growth phase. One of the most important things you need to do is be a visionary and inspire people to seek new and creative solutions to move the company to the next level. Growth can be exciting, but it also has its challenges. A leader must be able to articulate what the challenges are and where the company will be if they are solved. A great leader does not tell people how to solve the challenges but creates an environment where people want to roll up their sleeves and participate in the growth.

In contrast, during difficult times such as economic downturns or other crises, you need to focus on meeting those specific challenges. These are quite different than the positive challenges regarding growth. In crisis a leader needs to be mentally agile to help the organization evaluate the dangers. A leader must help the organization change course and redirect the company to find new opportunities.

When your competition is taking aim at your company to gain market share or you have a breakout product that needs to be launched immediately, then you must be quick thinking and courageous. You cannot sit back to consider every possibility, or you might lose valuable time. You can't play it safe and wait until you have analyzed every scenario. You must respond quickly to avoid missing out on important opportunities or losing market share that might never be recouped.

When business is going well and you are on a clear and stable path, you need to be responsible and discerning. You must be able to discern what got your company to this good place. Was it a lucky accident? Likely not. Was it a thoughtful decision with great execution? Once you know what the organization did well, then you can reinforce those systems, initiatives, strategies, and behaviors. You must take the time to strategize the next steps to keep the company fresh, vibrant, and moving forward into the future.

Passion is an ingredient that every leader needs to be effective, but any leader will tell you that passion at a constantly high level simply cannot be sustained. Passion by its very nature will spike as projects are launched, new customers are onboarded, and mergers or acquisitions take place. Passion is most effective when used in measure. A bit of passion applied at the right time can spark new ideas or revitalize a team. On the other hand, constant passion can feel frenetic to everyone around you, so maintain intervals of calm and directed work with times of increased energy and passion. One additional thing to note—if you are passionate about everything, people might begin to doubt your credibility and sincerity.

No matter what the situation, good or bad, focus is necessary. The things you focus on are the things that will get done. If you are focused on the future exclusively, you might miss actions that should be taken in the present. If you are only focused on today, you might miss important signals that the business or market is changing. A balanced focus will help you see your company's big picture.

Of course you will use other traits during the times described above, but some traits will be more useful in certain situations. Think of it this way. If you are making a recipe with lots of flavors, you have to balance them. At certain times, you might want one or more of the flavors to be dominant. When that happens, the other flavors are still there. They are just not as prominent. If any ingredient you are using is really strong—say, Tabasco sauce—you might want to use it in small measure so as not to completely overpower all the other flavors. If you turn up the heat and make it too spicy, the taste of what you are making might be overwhelmed.

This same principle is true about leadership traits. All the traits are important, and knowing when to emphasize one over the other is where balance comes in. You must intentionally create balance to achieve excellent results. Here are a few examples.

Compassion and empathy with regard to an employee facing a difficult life situation are great qualities. If your compassion leads to making a decision that is not in the company's best interest, then you are acting irresponsibly. Let's say an employee had a change in day care providers and had to leave early a few days a week. You allow that employee to do that for a short time while the situation gets resolved. However, the weeks drag on into a month, and it does not seem as if the employee is working very hard to find a solution. This puts the rest of the team in a bind because this individual's work is vital. As a leader, you must balance your desire to help this individual with your responsibility to keep the company healthy. You must develop a solution that serves both the employee and the company. If that is not possible, you must put the company ahead of the individual.

Additionally, if you are so focused on a problem or initiative that you are constantly down in the weeds, you might forget that you need be visible and inspire people. Without inspiration, the entire organization can slow down and lose the dynamism that is important for growth.

When you face a crisis situation and react too quickly, you might not discern some of the risks of your actions. Imagine you give approval to start a project. Employees begin to spend significant time and money on the effort. You then discover there are not legal safeguards in place, and sensitive information has been shared with improperly vetted individuals. They then share that information with your competitors. Acting too quickly in this case placed the company and its future in peril. While it is great to be quick thinking, you must balance this trait with discernment and thoughtful analysis.

We hope you begin to see that even good leadership traits in the wrong amounts can be detrimental. It also goes without saying that any of these traits are less effective if you are not visible to the teams you lead. In this era of digital communication, it is easy to avoid face-to-face communication. You can get lulled into thinking that e-mails and teleconferences are just as good as the real thing. Nothing could be further from the truth. It is difficult for digital communication to convey the passion you have for a project. For that, people need to see facial expressions and hear the intensity of your voice. Cute little smiley faces or frowns simply don't substitute.

Leaders must be walking the floor, communicating, and listening on a consistent basis. It is not enough to have a vision if it is not well communicated. Vision is not just a one-time event. You can't lay out a vision and walk away. People need frequent communication messaging to understand and engage in a vision.

When there is a crisis and leadership is critically needed, you cannot hide and hope someone else will respond. Sometimes leaders must be visible and work with people. Cynthia routinely goes into the office when employees work after hours on difficult projects. While she might not be able to do the tasks employees are performing, she can show support by being there and helping them think through issues and execute the vision.

A great deal has been written about balancing life and work. Just as it's important to maintain a work-life balance, you must also learn how to balance the traits that will make you successful as a leader.

Tips and Takeaways:

- The art of balancing leadership traits is a critical skill to master.
- Even good traits must be used in proper measure for the best results.
- A good leader should walk the floor and resist the temptation to rely on digital communication.

CHAPTER 9

DO YOU HAVE TO WAIT IN LINE?

Females are really good at waiting in line. Doreen has observed this tendency in her work with children. Little girls in classes wait patiently in line and follow their teachers' instructions. They rarely get out of line, cause distractions, or bother other girls in line. In contrast, little boys are not very good at waiting in line. They jostle for position, get out of line to cut in front of others, and don't really listen to their teachers' instructions. They are more focused on doing what they want to do—being first and being best. Doreen has also observed hesitant behavior in the adult women she works with in leadership development. Female professionals are prone to wait in line rather than jostling for position in the business world. They wait for someone to give them instructions instead of figuring out things on their own. They let others cut in line without saying anything. They don't want to draw attention to themselves or cause distraction for others. This is exactly the wrong approach for women who truly want to advance their careers.

The business environment is competitive because there are so many men in it, and men are competitive. That's not a bad thing, and it is the reality of the business world. So, women who want to succeed must learn to be competitive. This means not waiting in line.

There is often a progressive path that leads to leadership roles in a large company. An individual becomes a director or manager. That person takes on more and more responsibility and expects to move to the next level, but sometimes his or her progress becomes stalled. Sometimes that person is waiting for someone to retire or leave and go to another company. This is true for both men and women. However, research shows women are more likely to stall at the management level because they are willing to wait in line. In contrast, men are more likely to seek positions in other companies or advocate for other positions in their current companies if they believe their careers are stalled. They are not very good at waiting in line.

This process can be different in small businesses. Here women tend to move up faster, and it's not just because the organizations are smaller. We believe this has to do with the culture of smaller, more entrepreneurial firms. Often people are valued and rewarded for what they bring to the company—not necessarily how long they have served. In smaller companies, performance is noticed—not just potential. According to McKinsey & Company which is "a trusted advisor to the world's most influential businesses" men often receive promotions based on potential rather than performance.

However, no matter the size of the organization, there might come a time when you feel you are simply waiting in line. This is when women need to be aware of the female tendency to wait in line. If this is happening in your career, you will need to decide if the wait is worth it...or if you need to take action.

If you find yourself waiting in line, we recommend you ask yourself a few difficult questions.

- Are you waiting to be noticed?
- Are you afraid to raise your hand and say you want to move up?

- Have you asked outright what your potential is with the company?
- Have you communicated your goals in yearly evaluations to supervisors?
- Have you actively advocated for yourself at every opportunity?
- Have you built a résumé within and outside your organization?
- Have you shown you can be a strategic thinker?

If you have not been proactive about verbalizing what you want, men will cut in line and move ahead of you.

If you really want to get out front, you must strategically manage your career because no one will do it for you. Here are a few things you should start to do immediately:

- Don't let your résumé get stale. Keep it fresh. Continue to build it with new education, responsibilities, and experiences. Document your experiences and update your résumé, profiles on social media, and other materials.
- Read constantly. We know the old adage says opportunity favors the prepared mind. So, if you are reading about your industry, business trends, leadership, and other topics, you will be ready to engage and impress people in business conversations at all levels. You will be ready to seize opportunities when they arise and will increase your confidence to seek new opportunities.
- Subscribe to relevant blogs and websites. There are countless resources, and one is www.trendwatch.com. It is an innovative investment tool.
- Be aware of what is happening around you locally, regionally, nationally, and internationally. Understand current trends, cultural shifts, changes in the economic climate,

and other factors that will affect business in general and your industry in particular.

- Understand how your business is impacting customers—even if you are not directly a business that is customer facing. Everyone needs to know what customers expect and need from the business. Understand the needs of employees and colleagues as well. A leader cannot lead unless he or she has a complete understanding of the entire business supply chain.

- Maintain excellent health. You can't step up if you are not in peak physical and emotional health. If you are looking to move up and you have health issues or a lack of energy, it will certainly affect your performance. If you are not mentally healthy, it will affect your focus. Either one of these will put you at a disadvantage and keep you waiting in line.

Sometime women feel as if they are stalled, but they are actually causing these situations by choosing to be passive or not taking action. If you are standing in line and have been passed over a few times, assess your situation and begin to take action. You could be in the wrong company and might never progress from your current position. If this is true, you will need to evaluate what the right company looks like for you, according to your personal values and aspirations. You'll need to do some soul-searching and research and then begin your job search.

If you have been told you have potential but you are not being promoted, consider that someone might simply be telling you what you want to hear. If you have tried to progress on a number of occasions and have been told it is not the right opportunity or you hear other excuses, this could be a pattern of behavior designed to keep you in a job because you are helping your supervisor look good. That supervisor might try to appease you to keep you in the organization. You need to find someone who will be truthful with you. Hopefully, this person will tell you how to move ahead or if this is even possible. If it becomes obvious nothing is going to change in your current company, you have to face the reality that you might need to move on.

Another consideration is the timing—for the organization or you. You might think you are ready to advance, but wanting it does not necessarily mean you are ready. If this is the case, you will need to get some specific coaching on how to make the leap forward. It might also be possible your organization has timing issues. They might have individuals who have held positions for some time and the company has commitments to these people. They are not free to move them out of their positions—especially if they are older workers who might trigger discrimination problems. In this case, you will need to decide how long you are willing to wait.

If you decide to step out of line and out of your company, be realistic and plan carefully. The general wisdom is that it's easier to find a job when you have a job. That is the truth. Do not get mad and quit. Begin to research options, find a recruiter to work with, and use your network. Do your homework to be sure you don't find yourself right back in an organization just like the one you left. Conduct research to find the companies aligned with your values and aspirations and whose products or services you are passionate about.

- In interviews, ask questions aimed at learning more about the company, its culture, and its processes.
- Consider if you are in the right industry.
- Evaluate the culture of the potential organization.
- Talk to people throughout a potential organization—not just the leaders. You might get a very different picture when talking to those on the front lines.

Everyone stands in line at some point. However, you can get to the head of the line if you are proactive. Get out of line if the company is not the right fit for you. Take charge of your career so others don't cut in front of you.

Tips and Takeaways:

- Little girls are better at waiting in line than little boys, and this can continue into their work lives. Beware.
- The path to and strategy for leadership vary from a large organization to a smaller one.
- Timing is critical when it comes to advancement. That includes timing for the organization as well as the individual. Both must be in sync.

CHAPTER 10

HOW TO BE A LEADER MEN FOLLOW

Women sometimes complain they are not respected or taken seriously by the men in their organizations. They believe men try to undermine their leadership or simply will not follow them. Effective women leaders know how to behave so that everyone—men and women—will follow them.

To be a respected leader, you must be an expert not only in your field, but with regard to male-female dynamics. Let's explore some of the ways women operate that cause men to doubt their leadership.

We have all heard the term "queen bee." This refers to a strong performing woman who often works to eliminate weaker females or males in order to rule the workplace. Some women adopt this pattern of leadership because they want to feel powerful and in control. They believe that just because they are leaders, others should defer to them. After all, they reason, they are special. They believe they are forces to be reckoned with or powerhouses. When others show weakness or do not defer to them, they find reasons to make sure those people do not progress, or they get rid of them. Those left in these companies try to take cover or avoid the queen bees. They certainly do not willingly follow the queen bees. Queen bees are not leaders in reality. They are "bosses." They might command people to do their bidding, but people will never give their very best to queen bees. They will work with resentment and do just what is needed to keep the queen bees satisfied.

Another behavior that some women adopt is creating an old girls' club. Some women believe that men have had old boys' clubs for years and it is time to level the playing field. These women don't look at individuals for their performances but make decisions based on gender. They promote women who should not be promoted. They give women opportunities for which they are not well suited. They might be doing this in a misguided effort to help women achieve equality, but they are not exercising sound judgment. If the concept is wrong for men, then it is wrong for women too.

Another futile behavior is becoming the office mom. If you are naturally a giving and nurturing person, it is easy to make the mistake of bringing that into the workplace. Ask yourself a few questions to determine if you are an office mom.

- Do you try to make people feel good about themselves? Do you smile and reassure people? Do you coddle them?
- Do you feed people?
- Do you bring in treats?
- Do you delve into personal issues and give advice?
- Do you plan company events?
- Do you leave sweet notes for people?

These things are not off limits all the time, but if you are consistently acting like a mom, it is a problem. What grown man (or woman for that matter) wants to follow a mom around in the workplace? Behaving like a mom will inevitably damage your leadership potential.

The alpha female is at the opposite end of the spectrum from the office mom. However, it is also a dangerous trap for the woman who wants the men in her organization to take her seriously and follow her lead. The alpha female—much like the alpha male—tries to bully her way into the boardroom. This type of woman is a screaming bitch. Yes, we said the word every woman hates. Unfortunately, sometimes it is true. The alpha female tries to overpower others without listening to what they have to say. She is controlling and feels threatened by anyone else's success. Everyone hates this kind of person, and for men, it simply reinforces the belief that women cannot lead.

Being the queen bee, leader of the old girls' club, office mom, or alpha female is likely to subvert your efforts to reach the highest levels of your company, get the pay you want and deserve, and have men in your organization follow you wholeheartedly.

So, what should you do?

Be Authentic

To begin, you must be an authentic person. The word "authentic" is sometimes overused and misunderstood. It means to be genuine—not a copy of someone else, but real. In the context of leadership, being authentic means being true to your own values and style. Many women feel they must copy the leadership style of others—specifically men in their organizations. This is a huge mistake. When women leaders copy, it causes men to be distrustful. In the words of Shakespeare's Polonius from a scene in *Hamlet*, "To thine own self be true." It's also important you are the same person whether you are leading a meeting or chatting with someone in the break room. If you try so hard to create a persona instead of being yourself, you simply will not be able to do it for long. Soon you will be marked as a fake. If people believe you are a fake, they also doubt your knowledge and begin to question how you achieved your position.

Be a Company Woman

If you want men to follow, you must consistently have the best interests of the company and its employees at heart over your own interests and agenda. Most people have heard the phrase "company man." Over the years, that has gotten a bad reputation. What is wrong with being loyal to your company, though? What is wrong with executing the initiatives the company believes to be important? You need to be a company woman. When you see opportunities that will advance your interests and the company's interests, act! According to Global Entrepreneurship Monitor 2014 US report published in *Barron's*, "34% of women see opportunity and report that fear holds them back." You must have the courage to act if you want others to follow your lead.

Develop Unmatched Expertise

It is hard to argue with an individual who has developed a deep expertise. Most people respect a leader who is clearly knowledgeable. This is not to say you must be arrogant, but do position yourself as the one people can come to because you have done your homework. Men and women appreciate a leader who is the real deal.

Exercise Self-Discipline

You must also exercise discipline in your behavior and demeanor because everyone hates a screaming bitch—especially men. Always treat everyone with respect—regardless of the circumstances. This can be very difficult when men are trying to undermine you, get you to snap, or make you appear less than competent. When you lose control, you lose! In an era of smartphones and other devices, your every move can be recorded. One misstep can result in an unflattering video being shown countless times within your organization and maybe even going viral. We will talk more about that in an upcoming chapter that explores the topic of getting emotional.

Communicate Clearly

Communicate clearly what you want. Many women fall into the trap of looking at employees' work and saying, "That's not what I wanted." This is not helpful and gives men the opportunity to rant that they simply don't know what to do to make their leader happy—or that their supervisor is always changing her mind. Set specific, measurable expectations. Next, check that people understand these expectations, and then hold people accountable. When someone falls short, be instructive rather than critical. Don't say, "What were you thinking?" or, "You just don't get it, do you?" (By the way, you could be saying this with your facial expression and body language.) Instead, you need to ask questions to determine what went wrong and then offer some alternatives. Better yet, you should help that employee think through the options. Your clear communication will identify the bull's-eye so employees can hit the mark.

Back in the 1950s, Gallup starting polling about the preference for a male or female boss, and only 5 percent of Americans preferred a woman at that time. In 2014, 25 percent of women said they would prefer a female boss. This was compared to 14 percent of men. Women have made strides as leaders, but these statistics tell us there is still a long way to go—especially with men.

The stereotype of female leaders as bossy and difficult is alive and well. As a female leader, you must be aware that stereotypes will taint your actions. Work to be sure you are not reinforcing them.

Tips and Takeaways:

- Women can behave in ways that cause men to doubt their leadership abilities.
- Be careful you do not fall prey to becoming a queen bee or alpha female.
- Be an authentic person. Never try to copy someone else's leadership style.
- Never scream or yell.

CHAPTER 11

HOW TO BE A LEADER WOMEN FOLLOW

From the time girls are young, they are taught they are in competition with other girls. It is not the same kind of competitive spirit instilled in little boys. Girls are taught they must compete with other little girls regarding looks, personality, and talent. Last on the list is mental ability. Young girls are taught they must look good in order to get guys. Even after the feminist movement, this is still true. Women are rewarded for looks—not brains.

We hear much about needing more women in leadership, and while there is progress on this front, it is not significant enough for many. Sylvia Ann Hewlett studies gender diversity and business at Columbia University and is president of the Center for Talent Innovation. She is quoted as saying, "Having women leaders is not just a question of equity or somehow ticking the box. Particularly at technology companies, it really does contribute to innovation and a company's ability to exploit new markets." Women provide a diverse perspective that is a distinct advantage for every company. Some companies do recognize the value of women leaders and are making efforts to promote them.

So, what happens when a woman finally does break free of the constraints and use her ability to rise up in a company and become the leader? Surprisingly, it is often not what you think. Women who proclaimed that females needed to move up are suddenly jealous of other women's achievements. They start to pin the stereotypical labels to them. You hear them same things such as, "She was so great before she got that promotion, but now she is a nightmare to work for. She has changed. She is not like us anymore." You even hear the same derogatory terms men apply to women such as "queen bee."

What happens to all the support women supposedly have for other women?

To be fair, some individuals do not fit this mold. However, as we pointed out in the last chapter, male bosses are still preferred— even by most women. Perhaps women believe male bosses will be more helpful to their careers because men are seen as more powerful in the workplace. Women might believe male bosses will be able to help them progress faster because they will take them along as they get promoted. They might see male leaders as pro- tectors—people who will go to bat for them and take care of them when conditions at companies change.

Women might also subconsciously buy in to the stories about having a token female on staff. They might believe the company has promoted a woman and now it doesn't need more. If there is representation by a woman on the executive staff, then the com- pany has done what is expected today. It has met its quota, and there is not enough room at the top for two women.

Some women who ascend to the upper levels of management might be their own worst enemies because of how they lead. Maybe they sense the hesitancy of the women they lead or the outright disdain. They might try too hard because they want other women to like them. They might try to convince other women they have achieved their positions on their merits. What follows are some suggestions to lead effectively.

Be Yourself

To be a woman other women want to follow, you must do the very thing that scares you the most. Be yourself! Women have an uncanny way of knowing when another woman is not being authentic. They can tell when the woman is trying to be something she is not or puffing herself up. They sense when another woman is uncomfortable or ill at ease. Women want to see that their female leader is behaving in a manner consistent with the position she holds and her true self.

They want to get to know the real you and develop a relationship with you as a leader. You are not a friend and should never be a dictator or a pushover. You must be a real person who has the position because she worked hard and was qualified. You should exhibit all the qualities we discussed as the traits of a true leader and balance them as appropriate.

Be Evenhanded

Women want to be seen as equal to their male counterparts. They do not want to be treated differently. If you treat the women who work for you in a much different way than the men, even if it is better, that is not seen as positive. If you act as though you favor women, you will be doing yourself and all women leaders a disservice. You are also setting yourself up for failure with both men and women. Leaders who are not evenhanded will find every decision viewed as suspect.

Be Open Minded

Because women believe they are not heard as much as their male counterparts, you must remember to seek out women's opinions and then listen to them. Try to involve them in decisions that directly affect them. If they have been trained to fade into the background, you might need to encourage them to speak out at first. Don't dote on them, but do try to be welcoming to their ideas. You might choose not to follow their recommendations, but you do need to give them chances to contribute. Show you are open minded by asking thoughtful questions about their roles, their concerns, and possible improvements to make. Don't shut an idea down when you start to hear something you believe won't work. Hear them out, and you might be surprised. Most women and men simply want the chance to speak their minds. While many people are adverse to change, more and more they realize the need to try something new—a different approach or a fresh idea. Give them that opportunity, and they will follow you—even if the final decision is not exactly to their liking.

Manage the Change

If the women you now lead have never had a female leader, they might have a hard time with the change. People in general are resistant to change and this change could be a big one. Don't grumble and complain that your people don't want to accept a female leader. Do manage this change just as you would any other type of change. First, understand that change is difficult. Women will not accept a female leader overnight. You might need to have some patience at first. Try to understand the reasons for their behavior. Perhaps they have had bad experiences with other female leaders. Maybe they were hoping to get the job. It might be that they simply are not happy with where they are at, and it has nothing to do with you. You might want to address the elephant in the room. Ask directly what the issue is and have a frank dialogue. Don't be defensive if they say they simply don't like working for a woman. (However, most people will rarely admit this.) Explain calmly that you are leading this organization. Set the expectation that they will contribute and be as effective as possible. At some point, if an individual is not able to get past the issue, you will need to act decisively.

Women can be other women's worst critics and best defenders. How you approach the women you lead is critical to your success. If you do it well, they will be your champions. Do it poorly, and you will travel a bumpy road.

It seems odd that in this day and age we still need to talk about leadership in this segmented manner, but until there are more women leaders, this will be a topic for discussion.

Tips and Takeaways:

- Women who progress to the top levels of leadership might find other women are hesitant to follow them for a variety of complex reasons.
- It is critical you are evenhanded in your communication with men and women. Don't favor one over the other.
- You must manage expectations and understand the reasons behind the actions of women who challenge you. Then you will be able to address the issues calmly and without emotion.

Part 3: What Not to Do

CHAPTER 12

Getting Emotional

The now-famous song says, "Don't worry. Be happy." However, for many women, that is not as easy as it sounds. Women worry. They fret. They cry. They lash out. The truth is that men display some of these behaviors too…but these behaviors don't receive the same reactions from coworkers and superiors. When women display these behaviors, it plays into the perception that women are too emotional to make good leaders. This misperception is hurting many women as they try to climb the leadership ladder. This stereotype makes it important that women avoid getting emotional in the workplace.

So, here is some practical advice about what not to do.

Don't Cry

Imagine you are in a difficult situation. Someone criticizes your work or puts you on the spot. Someone questions your judgment. A common reaction is to feel hurt or get upset. Many women tear up and cry, as in this example from Cynthia Kay.

Cynthia sent Jane out to a jobsite to oversee a project for a client. Cynthia believed she could handle it, but she was uncomfortable and ill at ease. Before Jane returned, the client called and asked that she not be sent out again because they did not think she was as capable as others who had handled the work in the past. When Jane returned, Cynthia called her in to ask what had happened and told her about the client's comments. She sat and listened, and then it began. It was like a flood. She began sobbing and said it was not her fault. The young woman said the company had not prepared her well enough and that the client had obviously not liked her. She finished by saying that the job was simply not what she had expected. It was too hard. By the time Cynthia calmed her down, she was exhausted. Cynthia also knew this woman would never make it into a leadership position. Jane was way too emotional, and that made her irrational and ineffective.

An unfair double standard is that when men cry, they are viewed as sensitive. In fact, some people admire it in men, but when women cry, they are seen as weak. Some women use crying as a way to manipulate those around them. Some cry because they feel sorry for themselves or are frustrated because they don't know what to do. For women, crying will almost always harm your career aspirations. There are a few exceptions to this rule. If you are sincerely empathetic to someone's situation or are expressing gratitude, go ahead and get a bit teary.

Don't Lash Out and Get Angry

There is no place for explosive anger in the workplace. Actually, there are laws against a hostile work environment. Of course, there are degrees of anger, and in high-pressure situations, it is easy to say or do something you might regret. In plenty of movies, male bosses pound on the desk and yell at employees. While explosive anger does not work well for anyone, often men can get away with it. In contrast, no one likes an angry woman. In fact, when women consistently get angry, people avoid telling them things that might set off tirades. Employees might avoid sharing critical information, and this will ultimately undermine leadership. These leaders become isolated and miss the pulse of the organization. As result, their decision-making abilities are impaired.

Don't Vent

We all feel frustration—no matter what level you are at in a company. What you do with that frustration is important, though. Many women are tempted to vent. You do not have the right to do this. As a leader, you must stay in control at work with colleagues and superiors. You need to stay focused on what will move the company ahead—not what is frustrating you. You must be able to handle whatever comes your way with grace and poise. When you vent or unload, you are sabotaging your leadership.

Don't Let Worry and Anxiety Cloud Your Judgment

Women have been trained from the time they were little girls to serve and help others. In fact, many women try so hard to please everyone that they go overboard and try to give employees or coworkers everything they want. They worry about and cater to certain individuals instead of looking out for the greater good of their organizations. They also worry that those who work for them might not like them. So, they make decisions they believe will endear them to others instead of decisions that will move their organizations forward. When worry and anxiety cloud your judgment, you lose trust and respect as a leader.

Taking Offense and Acting Hurt

Many times, your judgments or actions might have been called into question. Perhaps you altered a production schedule. Maybe you restructured a team of people, closed down a facility, or authorized a new program. Then a superior put you on the spot to explain the action. Instead of responding in a thoughtful and measured manner, you took offense and acted hurt. You played the victim. "Don't you trust me? I don't understand why you are always questioning everything I do. Why won't you just let me do my job?"

Sound familiar?

Women sometimes fail to see that when they take offense to questions and sulk, they are not likely to get much support. This tactic might have worked with your parents, family, or significant other, but it is not effective in the workplace. Instead, make your case in a logical and concise way and then stop talking. Develop toughness and a new perspective. Remember, it is not personal. It is business.

So, why do women get emotional?

Contrary to popular belief, it does not have to do with the female brain. In fact, Daniel Amen in *Unleash the Power of the Female Brain* says women make better bosses because of the special strengths of their brains. He says, "Compared to men, women have larger volume in the frontal cortices and limbic cortices which is involved in many of the higher cognitive functions, including language, judgment, planning, impulse control, and conscientiousness, and emotional responses."

While we are not scientists, another answer is that women have learned to be overly emotional and react or withdraw instead of leveraging the unique structure of the female brain. Women are often given passes by their parents and families to act out and be emotional. Males are held to a higher standard, so they learn and practice emotional control from childhood. Developing emotional strength will take some practice, but you can do it.

Here are a few tips that work:

- Create some space and time to think. Walk away. This will help you avoid making a scene.

- Use self-talk. Tell yourself why it is important you think positively rather than negatively about a situation. Play out the scenarios in your head. What happens when you cry or get angry? What happens when you control that emotion and react in a healthy, positive manner? When you talk through a situation in your head, you are less likely to act out because you can see the results.
- Use a person you trust to help you gain perspective. This might be a coach or mentor. It could be colleague. One word of caution-choose this person carefully, or your struggle might end up as water-cooler talk.

Whatever strategies work for you, use them and practice gaining the emotional strength that it will take to get you through any situation. Your leadership potential depends on it. To start, take a few minutes and complete the following exercise. Advance preparation will help you demonstrate leadership when challenging situations arise in the workplace.

Exercise: What Would You Do Exercise

In each of the following scenarios, how would you handle the situation? What would you say? What tone of voice would you use? How would you manage your body language? What actions would you take to demonstrate good leadership?

- You have just pointed out an issue to an employee. She starts to sob.
- An employee is ranting and raving about having to work overtime in front of your team. You walk by just in time to hear them blaming you.
- An employee tells you about a co-worker who is planning to complain about you to the President of the company.

- In a meeting, a supervisor questions your productivity and commitment to a project that is behind schedule.

Tips and Takeaways:

- Getting emotional in the workplace is never a good idea.
- Women take offense and sometimes act out in ways that undermine their leadership positions.
- Reread our tips on developing emotional strength. Women can improve their emotional control with practice.

CHAPTER 13

OVERTHINKING YOUR DECISIONS

I t is definitely important to be thoughtful about decisions, but sometimes women take it to another level. They don't simply think about decisions and weigh all the options. They over-think even the smallest decisions. Have you ever seen a woman do the following when trying to solve a problem? She goes from person to person to explain the situation in depth. She tells the listener about all the different courses of action. She examines how each might play out and asks for feedback.

What is wrong with this? Everything.

This type of pattern says a lot about the person. Sometimes, a female leader simply does not want to take the chance of being wrong. She is afraid to take risks. She might fear being confronted if she makes a controversial decision. This demonstrates a lack of confidence.

Another problem is that many women spend so much time analyzing information and flip-flopping when making decisions that they become paralyzed. When you lead, you must be able to make solid, timely decisions.

This does not mean you should not ask for other opinions or collaborate with team members. Collaboration is good as long as you don't collaborate too much and get off track. If you consider too many possibilities, you will bog down the decision-making process. In today's warp speed business environment, you must stay on track. More importantly, you want to stay ahead of the pack. If you cannot make timely decisions, you might miss out on opportunities that others will scoop up.

Another pitfall that women experience is the desire to control every aspect of every decision. Some women are so controlling that people simply cannot do their jobs. You can't be a great leader and be controlling at the same time. In fact, if you are spending time controlling what others do, you are probably not doing the job you should be doing, which is making decisions that are critical to the growth and well-being of the company.

How do you avoid overthinking decisions?

First, understand that good decisions are based on information—not how you feel. You need to do your research, but here is an important thing to remember. You will never have 100 percent of the information you need. Even if you do, conditions change daily and sometimes hourly. So, ask yourself how much information you need to be comfortable. That varies with each individual, but a good rule of thumb is to gather 80 percent of the available information. That means you should focus on the most important content and just let some of the details go.

One approach is to break the decision down into smaller bites. Think of it this way. If you want to buy a new house, you generally don't just go out and purchase it. First, you get prequalified for a loan so you know how much buying power you have and if you will be able to secure funding. You might research neighborhoods. You might look at the property values, schools, and location with regard to essential services. Next you might look at the styles of homes, layouts, the number of bedrooms, etc. You are breaking the home-buying decision down into manageable decisions. This is the same process that can be used for business decisions.

Timing is important, and you must get that right. Once you have done the research, make the best decision you can. It might not be perfect. In fact, it won't be because nothing is perfect. If you wait for perfect conditions, you will never do anything. You will stall.

After you make a big decision, you might experience buyer's remorse. This is very common—especially with large decisions that impact people and the business in life-changing ways. Don't second-guess yourself. It is easy to feel as if you should or could have done more. Unfortunately, the world does not stand still, so you must be disciplined and keep moving forward—even if it feels scary.

One advantage of making a decision quickly is you can begin to test it out. Case in point, Doreen decided to open a satellite location for her sport recreation business. She did all the research and made the best decision she could make. The potential for this location looked excellent, and things actually got off to a good start. Customer growth, though, was not what it was expected to be. Those who did use the services there loved it. Staff loved the location and the new customers. The numbers did not work, though. It was a hard decision, but after twelve months, she closed the doors. By doing so, she avoided putting the business at risk and minimized the losses. Here is the critical lesson—you can re-verse most decisions if you go down the paths and find they are flawed. If you are going to fail, fail quickly.

Good old Honest Abe was a huge failure. Perhaps you remem-ber reading about Lincoln's attempts at business in history class. He evidently tried his hand at business and failed twice. In fact, he went bankrupt and spent seventeen years paying off the debt. He also lost quite a few elections before he won the presidency. Today, people say he was one of our greatest presidents and a true leader. The truth is you can do everything right and still fail. The important things are how you deal with failed decisions and what you learn.

Success is celebrated but failure offers the greatest opportunity for learning. The quote we noted earlier bears repeating. Winston

Churchill said, "Success is not final, failure is not fatal: it is the courage to continue that counts."

Don't overthink your decisions. Be bold. Dare to fail. You will learn a great deal.

Tips and Takeaways:

- To lead effectively, you must be able to make solid, timely decisions.
- Break large decisions into smaller bites so you can consistently be moving forward.
- If you are going to fail, fail quickly, and then work to find a different solution.

CHAPTER 14

USING UPSPEAK AND OTHER ANNOYING HABITS

As a leader, your behavior, language, and decisions are all under constant scrutiny. Sometimes the undoing of leaders is not over big things but the little annoying habits that cause people to question their credibility. Often these habits have developed over years and now are so ingrained that people do not realize what they are doing. Here are a few things that top the list of annoying habits.

Upspeak

Some have called it an affliction. Others say it is part of European language that has found its way into English. Still others say it is a trend that began on popular television shows that everyone from teenagers to adults is mimicking. Whatever it is, it is a commonly used speech pattern that works against those who are trying to lead. It is called upspeak, and it is a speech pattern that is more common for women than men.

Upspeak is the practice of taking a sentence that is not a question and turning it into a question. Therefore, the inflection at the end of the sentence goes up—hence the term "upspeak."

Think about these powerful questions. During President John F. Kennedy's inaugural address on January 20, 1961, he said, "And

so my fellow Americans ask not what your country can do for you-
ask what can you do for your country?" That speech and particularly this quote are cited time and time again. Even though this
idea is presented as a question, Kennedy's voice inflection actually
made it a statement. His voice went down at the finish of the sentence rather than up, giving the question power and strength.

Another famous example of a powerful question that has
stood the test of time is the opening of a soliloquy from William
Shakespeare's *Hamlet*. "To be or not to be, that is the question."
Again, the voice inflection goes down at the end and gives the
question power.

There is no doubt these are quotable questions, and they are
powerful thought starters. These questions are posed as challenges, and they were delivered with strength and conviction. In contrast, upspeak is the opposite. It turns a statement into a question
with the effect of softening what could be a strong statement. The
upspeak habit is more common in women because they are taught
not to be straightforward or too powerful in their language. Girls
are reprimanded for being bossy if their speech is too direct. So,
many females try to deliver a strong message but then sabotage
the effort by turning it into a question at the end of the sentence.

A carefully constructed and probing question can motivate
people to think about changing their behaviors, take a new course
of action, or stop to reflect. However, the consistent use of a questioning tone for a statement can have the opposite effect. When
used frequently, it becomes annoying.

Not surprisingly, female teenagers and women most often
use upspeak. Why? These are groups seeking reassurance. Think
about typical teens. They are unsure and trying to find their way in
the world. It is only natural they would look for validation.

There are many examples of Valley girls who use upspeak. "Do
you know what I mean? Like? Whatever?" This is great fodder for
comedians and parodies. Many mimic this and use it as a way to
add humor to even a business conversation.

What about women's use of it? Here the research is interesting. The College of William and Mary's Thomas J. Linneman conducted the most notable study. "Gender in *Jeopardy!* Intonation Variation on a Television Game Show" found that, "The more successful a man is, the less likely he is to use uptalk; the more successful a woman is, the more likely she is to use uptalk."

This might seem confusing, but it's not if you consider that many successful women feel they must apologize for or downplay their successes. How do they do that? By softening their language and using upspeak. A question is not nearly as forceful as a statement.

Consider the woman who is trying to establish a presence as a credible, competent leader. What makes her someone others choose to follow?

Leaders are people who have firm grasps of the world around them. They are people who possess the traits we discussed earlier. They are in the know. However, if every other sentence from a leader ends with an intonation that goes up, it signals a lack of leadership confidence. It seems as though the person is floating an idea or direction instead of confidently expressing why the idea is sound. We are by nature suspicious of individuals who flip-flop on ideas. We start to wonder: Why are they trying to find affirmation of their ideas or gather consensus before they take a stand? Don't they know enough? Do they not have the integrity to say what they think and stand by it?

Upspeak might be humorous when a Valley girl uses it, but when a professional uses it, it can sabotage communication. Avoid it at all costs.

Girl-Speak

Another verbal faux pas is something we refer to as "girl speak." There are two manifestations of this. The first is the choice of language. Playful, childish language does not reflect professionalism and should be reserved for personal conversations outside the workplace. This also applies to conversations that are excessively feminine or include exclusively female content. For example, talking about hairstyles and make-up. This includes girlie sounds such as "ooh" and "ah" or an excited girlie scream of delight or concern. Some women have been taught from a young age to speak this way because it supposedly makes them more feminine and appealing. Nothing could be further from the truth. Girl speak undermines a woman's leadership image and impact. A more effective strategy is to use powerful words, enthusiasm, energy, and passion. These are positive ways to get your message across. The second aspect of girl speak is tone of voice. Some women have a singsong lilt to their voices. Women's voices are also naturally higher and often considered less authoritative. Women should consciously lower their voices and monitor their patterns of speech so they are more direct. Girl speak—like upspeak—is annoying.

Lack of Eye Contact

Another annoying habit is the lack of making eye contact. In some cultures, the lack of eye contact is a sign of respect. However, in the business world, it is a huge red flag. It says you are uncomfortable with the subject. It might signal that you are not confident about your position. It might also say you are embarrassed about something—for example, your performance.

Have you ever walked down the hall at work and seen someone deliberately look way, pretend to be reading something, or pick up his or her cell phone? Most of us would interpret this as attempting to avoid communication. We might even think the person does not like us. If you are a leader, eye contact is critical. It says you are open to others, interested in what they say, and sure of what you are doing. Offer others the respect of looking at them during your conversations or during presentations.

One caveat is that too much eye contact is as bad as too little. If you fix your eyes on someone and don't break eye contact, that can be viewed as hostile or even condescending. If you have a piercing stare, it can be annoying and even a little scary. So, what is the right amount of eye contact? That varies depending on the situation. If you are listening intently to someone, you will have a lot of eye contact. If you are speaking face-to-face with a person, you will want to maintain good eye contact, but you might also look down occasionally to collect your thoughts. There is no hard-and-fast rule, but one way to judge if you are on target is to watch the other person's face. If he or she appears engaged and comfortable, you are probably doing a good job of maintaining appropriate eye contact. Eye contact is a critical element of social interaction, and the best leaders are adept at it.

Sexual Body Language

One of the things often parodied on television or in movies is the famous "head toss." It brings to mind a shampoo commercial. Have you noticed women who twirl their hair around their fingers? Constantly run their fingers through their hair or touch their faces? All these little gestures are subconscious body language that can be considered flirty or seductive. While these patterns might be fine if you are in a dating situation, they are annoying in the workplace. Use your hands to emphasize your message rather than using them to distract from it.

It is easy to develop habits. It is hard to break them. Develop awareness of things you say or do consistently. They might be distracting your colleagues and diminishing your power in the workplace. A helpful way to assess your habits is to watch yourself on video. You might be surprised at what you see, but it will help you see yourself as others do. We'll talk more about communicating with power in a later chapter.

Tips and Takeaways:

- Upspeak is the practice of taking a sentence that is not a question and turning it into a question.
- Using upspeak or girl talk works against those who want to lead.
- Be aware of body language, and use it to strengthen your communication.

CHAPTER 15

THE GENDER GAME

Even with heightened awareness and political correctness, gender is still an issue in the workplace. Discrimination can be overt. Just look at what was learned about Sony's discriminatory pay practices when it was hacked. In the entertainment industry, leading female actresses were paid significantly less than their male counterparts. In the business world, it is much the same. Discrimination does exist. While we will not spend any time discussing double standards or inequity, we will explore how women use or misuse gender in business.

How Women Dress

To be taken seriously, women must present themselves in a businesslike manner in dress, language, and behavior. Many women still have misconceptions about dressing for the workplace. It's no wonder. Take a look at what some women look like on the news sets of popular networks. Cocktail attire (even on morning programs) has replaced businesslike dress. Dresses have plunging necklines. They are skintight, and hems are short. It is obvious some women are using their appearance to grab ratings. It must work because more and more women are opting for the sexy look.

The same is true in the business setting. Using dress to get attention or manipulate coworkers or customers is nothing new. However, if you want to be known as a leader, turn off the subtle (or not-so-subtle) use of sexuality. This is not about grabbing anyone's attention. It is about business results.

This is not to say women should look dowdy or masculine. Dress can be sharp, trendy, and feminine without being provocative. Balancing this is an art, and for some it is a lost art. Beauty can't get you everywhere. Being intelligent, competent, and accomplished gets you further and keeps you in a position of leadership. Beautiful, sexy CEOs don't last long if they don't meet the expectations of investors and customers.

How You Behave

Playing the gender card is not just about how you look. It can apply to what you say and do. Some women use suggestive or flirtatious language to get attention. Don't. It can be misinterpreted. It can land you in HR for sexual harassment and put you in compromising situations. This is not to say a woman can't be funny and witty, but leave the sexual undertones out.

What You Do

Women do some other things in the workplace that can work against them. For example, some women always bake cookies or sweets and bring them in to coworkers. They use food as a way to get people to like them. They are always arranging social events. They plan the summer outing, the holiday party, and the Friday afternoon get-togethers. Women sometimes become caretakers in the office. That's fine if this is a role you want to take on. However, this will not help you gain the respect of your peers and supervisors and it won't enhance your leadership image.

Socializing in the business setting is another behavior that can send the wrong signals. Too much socializing makes you appear not focused on business. If finding out what your coworkers did over the weekend, where they shopped, or what their children are doing is more important than moving company initiatives forward, you will not be respected as a leader.

In most cases, this behavior simply reinforces the stereotypes of women in the workplace. These can range from the mom to the sex bomb. Neither one will help you move up to the C-suite.

An underlying problem is that women often want to have it both ways. Sometimes they use their sexuality to try to get noticed or move up, but then they complain they are being objectified. They want to take care of everyone, but they complain they are not being taken seriously.

Some women want to be treated preferentially. They want to have doors opened or have men rise when they enter a room. On the other hand, they want to be equals with their male counterparts. It's no wonder these mixed messages often confuse men. If they open doors and stand, they are criticized. If they don't do these things, they are criticized. Men feel as if they can't win.

As a female leader, it is important to be credible. You must stay focused on the business and be professional in every interaction. You must not take offense if you think you are not getting preferential treatment. This is what is required to ascend to the C-Suite.

Much has been said about the lack of women in the C-suite. As a result, many companies are under pressure to move women up the corporate ladder. These companies' shareholders, stakeholders, or customers have told them they need more women in upper management.

Are these opportunities for women to succeed? Maybe. Maybe not. There might be desire on the part of well-meaning companies to move women up for the right reasons. However, if a woman is simply filling a quota and does not have the skills to do the job, then it can end in failure.

When that happens, as it sometimes does, women might play the gender card instead of accepting they did not measure up to the levels of competence needed. Before promoting anyone, it is important to figure out if that person really has the skill set that business wants and needs.

The question a woman should ask is, "Am I getting in my own way by blaming others?" Business is business, so don't get distracted by personalities or feelings. Do a genuine assessment of your skills and ability to deliver results. If you have not done the hard work to move up the ladder or stay on top when you have been given the opportunity, don't whine or make accusations to coworkers that you have been mistreated or passed over. Don't go to human resources unless there is a real, quantifiable reason. The best strategy is to seek feedback that will increase your self-awareness and help you understand how you need to grow.

Yes, despite much progress in the business world, discrimination still exists. At some point, though, as a leader or potential leader, you will have to choose your battles and be very strategic.

Over the years, we (Doreen and Cynthia) have been in situations that were uncomfortable and discriminatory. In one instance, the vice president of marketing for a manufacturing company actually told Cynthia not to show up to the monthly update meetings. He "preferred dealing with a male business partner." He was an older white male who obviously had not paid attention to any discrimination training the company had provided. Cynthia did not back down. She did make a trip to his human resources department to report the incident, though. The HR director was concerned about some legal action being taken. Cynthia told the HR Director her concern was for the women who worked at this company. If the vice president acted this way toward a supplier, he was probably doing it to women in the company. That was the bigger issue. The next month at the monthly meeting, this vice president was not exactly cordial, but the atmosphere had definitely improved, and over time a very good working relationship developed.

When Doreen wanted to sell a building she owned to move into a larger building, she looked for a logical buyer. The same man owned the buildings on either side of hers, so she approached him to see if there was interest, and there was. However, he asked Doreen to have her husband call him to discuss the details. The problem was Doreen's husband was not involved in her business, and, of course, she was perfectly capable of handling it. In response to this roadblock, she called her commercial real estate agent. The agent listed the building, and it sold within a week. Doreen could have sat around whining about being mistreated or dismissed. She could have asked her husband to make the call. She did not even consider those options, though. She did what capable leaders do—get the job done. One of our favorite mantras is that if we can't go through people, we go around them. We can't tell you how many times we've had to do this in business, but we think sweet success is the best revenge!

Invariably there are situations where individuals will say discriminatory things. "I would rather work with a man" or, "We have to find a woman to fill the spot." Both of those are discriminatory against a gender which means society has not progressed as far as many think. Both Doreen and Cynthia have been invited to join a number of boards—not because of talent but because those boards needed female representation. Some might have been offended. They were not.

Instead, each directly asked the pertinent question. "Are you inviting me because you need a woman on the board? Do you need more diversity? A woman's perspective?" Sometimes faces got red, and the stammering started. Other times, there was the honest recognition that they were looking for female representation. That was a positive sign.

So, what is the ideal situation? It would be a world where we discard gender and focus on competency and confidence and working in diverse settings. We do not think of ourselves as female leaders or a term we both hate, "woman-preneurs." We think of ourselves as leaders. Period.

Many men are suspicious of exclusively female organizations because they think there is a great deal of male bashing that occurs. Rather than seeking exclusively female organizations, we suggest targeting and networking with groups where you have common interests and that include men and women who have achieved levels of success. We believe it is counterproductive to exclude any group and recommend you develop a diverse network and experiences.

The topic of gender is a difficult one, and all professionals have stories to tell of how their lives and careers have been impacted. They were promoted because of gender. They were passed over because of gender. They got chances or did not get chances because of gender. The research on gender discrimination in the workplace is exhaustive and shows evidence that it affects both men and women. Most of the research, however, says women are most often passed over. Women might not be considered for jobs that are physically demanding—such as police work—because some believe they cannot do the job. Men, on the other hand, might have difficulties getting into careers that are traditionally female such as nursing or childcare. The research also shows that both men and women use their gender for personal and professional gain.

Playing the gender game is risky for both men and women. The best course of action is to always be businesslike and professional in your dress and actions. If you find yourself in a place where that is not appreciated or rewarded, it is time to start looking elsewhere.

Tips and Takeaways:

- To be taken seriously, women need to present themselves in a businesslike manner.
- Do a real assessment to see if there is a gender bias in your workplace or if you just perceive there is discrimination.
- Discrimination still exists, but as a leader or potential leader, you have to choose your battles and be very strategic.

PART 4: WHAT TO DO

CHAPTER 16

BE A STRATEGIC THINKER

W e hear the word "strategy" used often in the business world, and strategic thinking is absolutely essential for anyone who aspires to be a Level Three Leader. This is a different way of thinking than a tactical approach. Tactical thinking is simple executing tasks and responsibilities and not necessarily connecting this to the big picture.

So, you might wonder, "What exactly is strategic thinking, how do I know if I have it, and is it an ability I can develop?" Yes, all people can certainly improve their strategic thinking abilities. Just like anything else in life, your ultimate skill level depends on your innate abilities and how much time and effort you spend learning, accessing resources, and practicing strategic thinking.

By definition, having a strategy means developing a plan of action designed to achieve a goal or overall plan. So, strategic thinking means you are spending time thinking about where to go and how to get there. Strategic thinking is complex—much more complex than just constructing some ideas in an hour or two for the purpose of achieving a goal. Strategic thinkers are thinking *all* the time. The best strategic thinkers actually never stop thinking because they can't. Their brains thrive on processing new information, sifting and sorting this information, and piecing it together with what they already know. Strategic thinkers are constantly thinking about the big picture, and they continually modify their visions with the new information they receive every day. They are flexible and creative as they gather new information.

Strategic thinking is a little like working a jigsaw puzzle. The first step in doing a puzzle is to look at the box top. That's the big picture or vision. This helps people visualize what they are constructing, and it helps them show the picture to the other people they are working with. Next, they begin constructing the edges of the puzzle—identifying the important boundaries and parameters to further define the big picture. Finally, they begin filling in the middle as they search for similar colors and patterns in the different areas of the puzzle. Strategic thinking is the same process. Strategic thinkers keep gathering information that will help them and others define and construct successful outcomes. They are always looking for puzzle pieces needed to successfully construct the big-picture vision.

Strategic thinkers do share common qualities that contribute to their mental agility and successful outcomes. They also continue to improve their strategic thinking by practicing behaviors that empower them to comprehend and apply complex information. The outstanding qualities of strategic thinkers are:

1. Being Curious

Strategic thinkers want to know how things work and what makes them work. They aren't satisfied until they understand at a deeper level than most other people. They are explorers and discoverers who bring their discoveries back to their teams or projects, and they use the new information to improve, challenge, and change outcomes. Strategic thinkers will turn over every rock and examine every crack and crevice to get to answers. They are not satisfied with "I don't know" or "this is close enough." Because their brains are constantly at work analyzing and questioning, they must go beyond talking about symptoms and get to core issues, causes of problems, and solutions. You can become more curious by questioning what you assume or think you know. Ask questions to get at the "why" and "how" of things. Ask questions to deepen your understanding, and don't assume you already understand.

2. Being Aware

Strategic thinkers are on constant alert. They have a higher level of awareness than most other people, and they pick up clues and information others might miss. They notice subtle shifts and trends in everything from culture and economy to attitudes, body language, and innuendos. Because of their acute awareness, strategic thinkers notice both overt and covert messages, and they apply this information to whatever problems and solutions they are working on. You can become more aware by practicing the art of paying attention to details about people and circumstances. Take the next step from seeing the details to interpreting them and thinking about what they mean. Think about how you would apply this information to enhance what you already know.

3. Being Perceptive

Strategic thinkers perceive more deeply than most others. Because of their active levels of thinking, they seek to assign meaning to behaviors and situations. They analyze at deeper levels to increase their understanding. They connect previously learned information with new information to enhance their perceptions. Strategic thinkers might think about interactions or situations for days until they can better understand what they mean—and more importantly what they mean to them, their organizations, their goals, and their values. You can become more perceptive by spending more time thinking about things that previously puzzled you. Think, reflect, and ask until you gain a deeper level of understanding.

4. Being Connected

Strategic thinkers are constantly seeking new information to help them plan, organize, and communicate in order to move initiatives forward. They are voracious readers. They are lifelong learners who are connected to colleagues, community, educational organizations, their industries, the arts, the business world, world news, their families, their friends, etc. They are constantly seeking to connect because it provides new information, new thoughts, and challenges to their previous thinking. This interconnectedness helps strategic thinkers check their own assumptions by sharing them with others, and it helps them gather new information through listening to conversations and presentations. They genuinely value the thoughts and ideas of others and seek to enhance and challenge themselves through their relationships with others and the world at large. You can become more connected by increasing your scope of influence and interaction. Reach out to new groups and individuals—particularly those who seem different than yourself. Diversity promotes the most meaningful growth.

5. Being Open

Strategic thinkers don't need to be right. They don't need others to agree with them, and they actually like it best when people don't agree. This is when they are on high alert—when their theories and opinions are put to the test. Strategic thinkers are open to every viewpoint and enjoy the process of proving or disproving a theory or plan. They are open to input regardless of where or whom it comes from. They listen to people from the CEO to the custodial staff and everyone in between. They believe great ideas can be found everywhere, and they have no need to own all the answers themselves. Strategic thinkers believe greater involvement creates the best solutions and results. You can become more open by placing yourself in situations that might make you uncomfortable. Be with people who know more than you do. Be with people you think might know less than you do. Be with people you perceive as different from yourself. Be open to all kinds of new situations without prejudging.

6. Being Balanced

Strategic thinkers create life balance and make time for themselves. Even though they are always thinking, they are not always working. They take time to be with friends and family. They schedule time for recreation and relaxation. They care for their bodies and minds to keep them in top condition. Strategic thinkers often fit the "puzzle pieces" together best when they are relaxing—on vacation, during jogging or walking, in conversation with friends, while reading, etc. Strategic thinkers understand that constant work and stress inhibit their abilities to think clearly and creatively. So, they intentionally create time for new ideas to simmer and the best solutions to bubble to the top. They don't feel guilty about making time for themselves because they understand it benefits everyone—their companies, employees, families, friends, and themselves. They consider the big picture and greater good rather than allowing themselves to be slaves to the tyranny of the urgent. You can be more balanced by scheduling time for relaxation. Be sure this is true relaxation when your mind can be at rest. These are the best times for the "light bulb" to go on, to find solutions to problems that might have previously seemed puzzling.

7. Being Creative

Strategic thinkers look for all kinds of ways to tinker. This means they look at problems from all perspectives and try all kinds of things. They don't discount ideas until they have thoroughly considered every way they could possibly work. They invite others to engage in the process and offer new ideas and ways of doing things. They know that sometimes the best solutions come from failure and roadblocks, and they are especially alert when things seem not to be working out. They are not discouraged by what seem to be dead ends. Instead, they keep working toward new breakthroughs. They are hopeful and helpful when the going gets tough, and they do not give up. Because of their curiosity, awareness, perception, connectedness, balance, and courage, they recognize creative solutions that others might miss. Their strategic thinking empowers them to connect the dots and create pathways not seen by others. You can become more creative by approaching problems with no preconceived ideas. Create as you go. Let go of the need to see the end, and engage fully from the beginning of problem solving with an optimistic and creative attitude. Stay open to every new idea and where it might take you.

8. Being Brave

Thinking strategically takes courage because it involves risk. Developing a great strategy necessitates wrong turns, false assumptions, letting go of ego, elevating other people's ideas, and failing. It is scary not to have the answer and not know the end result. The process of strategic thinking means you are in no-man's-land for a while as you seek new information, process it, and piece it together. Strategic thinking is not for the faint of heart. Strategic thinkers are not perfect and don't need to be. They just want to figure things out for the very best results. They also don't apologize for not having all the answers. They are OK with being criticized or misunderstood during the process of problem solving. They brave-ly push forward because they know that is the only path to suc-cessful outcomes. They don't give up any quest because they are scared or because of criticism. Concern for their organizations' greater good and people fuels their bravery. You can become more courageous by immersing yourself in strategic thinking and solu-tions rather than worrying about what other people might think about you. Start caring more about the outcome, and focus less on yourself.

9. Being Focused

Strategic thinkers filter out distractions and stay focused on the process and outcome. They don't get thrown off track by naysay-ers, office noise, demanding people, scare tactics, threats, or a host of other distractions. They stay on the trail like hound dogs. They hunt for clues and information to keep moving forward. If they can't go through people, they go around them, but they figure out ways to keep going. Temporary setbacks do not discourage stra-tegic thinkers. They see those for what they are—simply detours on the path to success. Because of their ability to stay focused, strategic thinkers can be labeled as uncaring because they don't engage in small talk, gossip, criticism, or a host of other office behaviors. They filter out any behaviors or interactions that are counterproductive to achieving goals. You can be more focused by intentionally removing yourself from office gossip and other coun-terproductive behaviors. Engage in conversations that help move ideas forward and create solutions. Be intentional in directing dialogue to problem solving and ideas rather than talking about people.

Nurturing the attributes above will help you become more stra-tegic in your own thinking. It will move you from being reactive to proactive. It will increase your ability to anticipate change as you become more aware and perceptive. You will identify more possibilities and be less restricted by prejudging your thinking or the thinking of others. You will enhance your agility and response to new ideas and trends. You will increase your wisdom as you combine new learning with long-held beliefs. You will become more patient with yourself and others. As a result, you'll be a powerful force in creating the future through strategic thinking.

All true leaders think strategically and must continue to improve their strategic thinking as they move into higher-level leadership. If leadership is your aspiration, begin to practice and hone the necessary strategic thinking skills. It is never too early to start. You can teach children in your life to be strategic thinkers by helping them learn the skills described in this chapter. It could help them become future leaders!

Tips and Takeaways:

- There is a huge difference between being tactical and strategic in your thinking. Leaders move from being tactical to strategic in their thinking.
- Strategic thinkers gather information that will help them and others define and construct successful outcomes. They are always looking for puzzle pieces needed to successfully construct the big-picture vision.
- The mental agility needed for strategic thinking can be improved with practice.

CHAPTER 17

COMMUNICATE WITH POWER

M any people have heard that being able to tell a story is one of the most important communication skills. That's true, but we believe powerful communication can be boiled down even further to the words used. Some words are clearly more powerful than other words, and women tend to use "softer" words and too many words. An important skill for female leaders to develop is communicating powerfully and concisely.

In many cases, it goes back to when women were young. Girls are taught to be nice, act like ladies, and avoid being direct. Straightforward women can be criticized for being too direct. Conversely, men and boys are rewarded for being direct straight shooters. Communicating with power is the mark of an inspiring and influential leader—male or female—and it is something everyone can learn to do.

Let's examine the power of the words we use.

Power words are those that are short and active. They evoke emotion and paint a picture. Choosing words that do all that is a tall order, and it takes practice. One thing is sure—some words scream power and create stronger impacts when you want others to hear your message. It is the difference between merely being descriptive and powerfully heightening awareness and calling one to action. Here are a few examples to get you started:

Descriptive: serious situation.
Powerful: catastrophe, horrific mistake.

Descriptive: fast.
Powerful: frantic.

Descriptive: safety issue.
Powerful: hazardous.

Descriptive: let people go.
Powerful: fired.

In difficult situations, people sometimes want to soften the news. However, if your team must take swift action in response to a crisis, powerful words will communicate the urgency and stir the emotions that fuel a quick response. Here are a list of words we think are powerful and can be used in disastrous (that was one!) situations.

- Nightmare
- Fail
- Unimaginable
- Critical
- Emergency
- Fight for survival
- Struggle
- Angry

Each of these words conjures up a picture. A power word immediately gives a clear, concise image of what the speaker or writer is trying to convey. One of the powerful phrases we remember from television was from the open to a sports show. "The thrill of victory. The agony of defeat." That phrase used power words to create emotion and connect with viewers.

Recently GM had to deal with a crisis regarding ignition switches. CEO Mary Barra addressed employees at a town hall meeting. The text of her speech was printed in *USA Today* on June 5, 2014. It read, "I realize there are no words of mine that can ease their grief and pain. But as I lead GM through this crisis, I want everyone to know that I am guided by two clear principles: First that we do the right thing for those who were harmed; and, second, that we accept responsibility for our mistakes and commit to doing everything within our power to prevent this problem from ever happening again."

That one paragraph has a number of power words throughout. Here it is again with those words underlined.

"I realize there are no words of mine that can ease their <u>grief</u> and <u>pain.</u> But as I lead GM through this <u>crisis</u>, I want everyone to know that I am guided by two clear principles: First that we do the right thing for those who were <u>harmed</u>; and, second, that we accept <u>responsibility</u> for our <u>mistakes</u> and commit to doing everything within our power to prevent this <u>problem</u> from ever happening again."

This was a very sobering and somber speech, and the words reflect that.

When the situation is a positive one, there are also power words you can employ. In this case, consider some of these:

- Amazing
- Bold
- Delightful
- Impressive
- Inspired

- Magical
- Marvelous
- Propelling
- Phenomenal
- Sensational
- Valuable
- Vibrant

When you want to inspire people, try some words like these:

- Authentic
- Controversial
- Energizing
- Fervent
- Guaranteed
- Idea-rich
- Instantly
- Passionate
- Relevant
- Profitable
- Proven
- Reinvigorated
- Responsive
- Secret
- Soaring

The purpose of your business communication varies, and the power words used should match your intent. That means you must consider what you are trying to do. Do you want to inform your audience or colleagues? Are you trying to convince someone to follow your recommendations? Do you want to exert influence, change behavior, or reinforce behavior? Do you want to recognize the efforts of a team that has done sensational work? Are you trying to encourage a team that is not measuring up? Do you want to excite people about a major initiative that will propel or catapult the organization forward? The list goes on, but what's important is that you understand exactly what you are trying to achieve. That way, you can use the most powerful words.

Think about inspirational leaders you have seen in the media. How do they capture your attention? They certainly are not boring. According to a Meetings in America study, a whopping 91 percent of individuals surveyed admitted to daydreaming during meetings, and 39 percent admitted to falling asleep. If you want more attention, be more interesting! Use power words. Then remember to use an important technique we call "cueing the listener." This alerts the listeners that they should perk up their ears. Examples of cueing the listener are statements such as:

If you only remember one thing…

Here's the critical point…

Let me repeat that…

Every one of these statements cues people to listen. It alerts the listener that what you are about to say is consequential. Overusing this technique or using too many power words can, of course, have the opposite effect. If everything is "amazing" or if every other word is a power word, it is overstimulating, and people turn off. However, because most people don't use power words, you will probably have to go a long way to overuse them. If you need help finding power words, it is pretty easy. Use Google to find synonyms that have more spice, more punch, and more vivid imagery than the word you intended to use.

There is a good deal of research about the use of power words, and it reveals that most people do not know how to find and use power words. That is why many people find themselves listening to a leader and thinking:

- There is nothing new here.
- I have heard this all before.

- I am so bored.
- I am wasting my time listening to this.

Most people have been in lackluster meetings. Chances are, with a little effort and a few power words, the results could have been dramatically different.

While we are focusing on words, we should also note that some power words are so overused that they have lost their impact. Here are a few words we suggest you limit or avoid using altogether:

- Awesome
- Breakthrough
- Collaboration
- Innovation
- Miracle
- Partnership
- Revolution
- State of the art

Another problem prevalent in communication is the use of too many words. Period. It is a common misperception that more is better. People, especially women, confuse the length of the communication with its importance. Work to eliminate wordy phrases. Make communication meaningful, shorter, and active. In other words, say it simply. Here are a few examples:

Ineffective	Effective
a large number of	many
A total of 102	102
advance planning	planning

bring the matter to the attention of	alert
consensus of opinion	consensus
is in an operational state	running
individuals who will participate	participants
firm commitment	commitment
newly created	new
obtain an estimate of	estimate
the reason why is that	because
was in communication with	talked to
with the exception of	except
make a decision	decide
on a national basis	nationally
never before in the past	never
in some cases	sometimes

Research affirms that a single word—when used appropriately—can make all the difference. Why then do we continue to use more words than necessary? Some of this is conditioning. Women are taught to explain themselves and be sure everyone understands exactly why they are doing things. Women also look for approval and make excuses for their behavior in order to gain that approval. All of that takes a lot of extra words. It also turns the listener off. It can overwhelm people, and they can't discern what to pay attention to in the barrage of words.

A communication professional who was a well-respected coach used to say, "Be brief. Be bright. Be gone!" Make your point. Then stop talking!

Exercise: Power Language

The use of power words in short, concise statements or probing questions is the mark of a good leader. This takes some practice, so here are a few example phrases to simplify. Try to rewrite these with power words to be more concise:

1. Our employees are our most valuable asset because they provide the company with the insight and creativity to move us ahead and compete with our competitors head-to-head and win the job.
2. We have been able to produce significant long-term results that have improved our ability to deliver products needed for short runs or special orders.
3. The range of services that our company provides is comprehensive and broad enough to provide maximum efficiency for our customers when they need a variety of products in a hurry.
4. Understanding your customer's needs just as much or more than your customer is vital to building a long, successful relationship—especially in these difficult and demanding times.
5. Suppliers can be our most-trusted and important partners but only if we have the opportunity to build relationships that are meaningful and profitable to everyone involved.

Another important aspect of communicating with power is the ability to ask a provocative question. A great leader does not need to know it all. Accept now that you simply cannot know it all. However, if you can listen to others and ask questions that get everyone thinking (or thinking differently), then you are seen as an insightful person. The best communication is a beautiful blend of interactions. Asking great questions shows you are a thoughtful leader who is confident enough to be interested in other viewpoints.

Whether it is asking a question, facilitating a meeting, or delivering a presentation, communicating with power is a must. Those who learn to communicate with power will influence others and excel.

Tips and Takeaways:

- Communicating with power is the mark of an inspiring and influential leader.
- Some words are more powerful than others.
- Women often confuse the length of the communication with its importance. Eliminate wordy phrases.

CHAPTER 18

CHANGE WHAT YOU CAN CHANGE

The world is constantly changing. One day you are using a certain set of tools. The next day they are obsolete. One month we value a particular employee skill set. The next month a different set of skills are required. One year the company is focused on a set of initiatives. The next year market changes necessitate a course correction.

Heraclitus, a famous Greek philosopher who was active around 500 BCE, was well known for his theory that things in the world are constantly changing. His famous quote is, "The only thing that is constant is change." This is still true today. However, even a small change is still the most difficult thing for an organization or people.

People often hear, "That's just the way it is." or our least favorite, "If it isn't broken, don't fix it." In many companies, the status quo is something to be protected. These organizations often spend time and energy trying to make sure everything is stable. They find unsettling anything that causes them to think differently or change processes or structures.

One of the most important things a leader can do is believe that change is possible, embrace it, and then work to engage employees.

Embracing change means leaders must understand that business today is in a constant state of change. They must be positive about what change can do for their organizations instead of dreading it. Markets are always expanding and changing. While much has been said about globalization over the years, it is finally becoming a compelling reality. Technology continues to change the way people work and communicate. The demographics of organizations are changing. Workforces now span from Millennials to the Silent Generation.

As a leader, you have a defined sphere of influence. It might be your direct reports, team, department, or even whole company. Within that sphere, you need to understand what you can change and what might be outside your influence.

Change does not occur unless leaders drive it. That does not mean employees are not important to the process. They are and should be engaged early when changes are imminent. Unfortunately, too many would-be leaders are passive. They know change is required, but they wait for someone else to do it. You might hear this type of leader say things such as, "I can't believe they can't see that. Why aren't they doing anything about this situation?" This passive leader is actually looking for others to lead change instead of strategically driving change. Remember, people can't follow unless you lead with strategy, vision, and passion.

Another sign of a passive leader is that the leader does not seize an opportunity to make things better. Instead, this person floats ideas and then waits for someone else to react.

It's a good idea to understand the difference between being active, proactive, and reactive. Some leaders are active but not really leading. They look around at their organizations to see what others are doing, jump on the bandwagon, and actively take part in the change. This is a mediocre place to be as a leader because the leader is participating but not leading change.

Some leaders are reactive. These people wait until situations are dire. They only react when it becomes clear they must do something. This type of leader actually becomes part of the problem instead of creating solutions.

Proactive leaders look at their spheres of influence and proactively set about making the necessary changes. This gets these leaders out ahead of others. These leaders become models and gain the respect and trust of their teams.

If you intend to lead, then you must understand your position in the company and the realm of control in that position. Start with questions about your role.

- What activities or initiatives am I directly responsible for?
- On what teams do I play key roles?
- Do I have a sphere of influence? Where and how can I influence?
- Have I been asked to help initiate a change, modify, or do a course correction for my team, department, or company?
- Have I earned others' trust and respect?

Once you have determined your role, you should also assess the expertise you have that makes you qualified to influence change. Ask yourself a few questions about your abilities.

- Do I have some unique talent?
- Do I have specialized knowledge or training that can be leveraged to lead change in my company, department, or specific project?
- Do I have a skill or have I achieved proficiency in a specific area?

It is your responsibility as a leader to make a contribution and bring appropriate solutions or improvements to the table. To do this, you need to make an honest assessment of how you are viewed within your organization. Try to see yourself as others see you. Ask yourself these questions:

- What is my company's perception of me? Is it accurate?
- Am I seen as a person of integrity?
- Am I seen as a thoughtful person and an innovator?

Once you understand your role, your abilities, and how you are perceived, try to figure out the best way to approach the change. Do you need to test it with your supervisor? Should you take it to a leadership committee? Do you have access to the highest levels of leadership at your organization—the CEO, COO, and CFO?

Leaders are in positions to see what programs are not working or when their organizations are making promises and not delivering. Often bad situations go on for years with no one taking action. If this is happening in your company, it is an opportunity for you to demonstrate your leadership by creating solutions and driving change. It's important to know that people get what they tolerate, so don't tolerate dysfunction. How do you change what you can change? Ask yourself a few more questions.

- What is in my control? What is beyond my control?
- Am I directly or indirectly responsible for this initiative?
- Is this work impacting work I am already doing?
- Am I being judged or evaluated by this work?
- Do I have influence in this realm?
- Is this in my area of knowledge or expertise?
- Do I have a unique skill set that empowers me in this situation?
- Am I complaining about the same things over and over instead of leading?

Every workplace has things that need to be changed or updated. If you remain passive until you are frustrated or agitated, you've waited too long. Leaders don't wait for negative emotions such as anger or frustration to motivate them. They regularly change what they can change. Leaders are determined to act when they see things that need changing. Leaders act on behalf of their companies because they know change is for the greater good—even when it is challenging or difficult.

What is the best approach to achieve the necessary change? A direct approach is often the best one. Be diplomatic and politically savvy in your process. Ask yourself these questions:

- What is the timeline for the necessary changes?
- How much influence and energy can I spend to make the changes?
- What are the consequences if I am not successful?

Keep in mind that even positive changes make people uncomfortable. Learning to navigate change is an important part of a leader's job, and sometimes leaders must go around people to effect change. This can be risky, so you should be realistic about whether you can really implement effective change in your company. If the answer is no, then the core values and processes of the company might not be aligned with your own. Don't quit immediately, and don't burn bridges, but do start looking. It might be time for you to make a career change.

Tips and Takeaways:

- Change is a reality. Embrace it.
- Great leaders are proactive rather than passive or reactive.
- Assess what is within your power and influence to change. Spend your energy and resources where you can be most effective.

CHAPTER 19

QUIT BEING BORING: LEAD WITH STYLE

Not everyone can or wants to be a charismatic leader, but everyone can lead with style. People want and need to be impressed by their leaders. If a leader does not exhibit a sense of excitement, a sense of urgency, and a passion for the work and company, why should anyone else? Some leaders are perfectly knowledgeable, strategic, and (unfortunately) boring. These leaders will never be able to progress to the highest levels because they don't know how to wow their organizations and people. So, what does it take? Figure out what makes you different and unique and own it. As a society, we spend a lot of time trying to fit in and be like everyone else. The media is full of celebrities competing to be popular. The nation is full of people following these celebrities and trying to be like them. It is uncomfortable to put yourself in a place where you are not following the crowd, saying what most people say, or acting like most people act. However, you will never really reach your true potential if you follow others. You must find and follow your own path based on your unique talents, passions, and perspective. To discover yourself and become more self-aware, ask yourself these questions:

- What do I do in a unique way?
- What is my unique set of talents and skills?

- Are there some quirky traits I have tried to suppress?
- Have I ever been told I have an interesting perspective?

You must discover what it is that makes you...you. You can't be someone else or copy someone else's style, and you shouldn't even try. It is wasted energy because you are not anyone else. You must discover what naturally attracts others to you. As you learn more about your personal appeal, attributes, talents, and contributions, you need to figure out how to tell your story in an engaging way. Think of yourself as a salesperson. This might be difficult if you have never thought of yourself that way, but essentially everyone is selling something all the time. Perhaps you are selling yourself so you can get promoted to the next level of leadership. Perhaps you are selling an idea. Maybe you want to persuade others to contribute to a program or initiative.

To lead with style, you must be able to tell a story effectively and communicate with powerful words and passionate energy. What are the faux pas of boring leaders, and how can you avoid them? Below we've listed some mistakes we have observed in boring leaders and some tips on how to avoid these foibles.

Boring: Use Corporate Speak

Leaders who use lots of jargon, overused phrases, and meaningless words in an effort to appear important are not effective. As a leader, if you are simply spouting the same things everyone else is saying in the same way, there is nothing to set you apart. Many times leaders use corporate speak because they believe it makes them sound smarter and more important. They say things such as, "We're focused on the future. We're working in collaboration with groups across the enterprise to secure our place in the industry. We must be transparent in all aspects of our operation so we can be operationally excellent and leverage best practices."

The problem is that phrases such as these could apply to any company anywhere. They are general statements that lack vision, passion, energy, conviction, and imagination. If your employees feel you offer nothing new and you do not present anything that challenges them, then you risk losing their attention and engagement.

Interesting: Use Your Own Words—Simplify

Eliminate overused and meaningless phrases. Think about what you are saying, and ask if you are trying to make it overly complicated or puffed up. If it is just the same old thing, then don't say it. If it is something that needs to be addressed, then use your own words. (For guidance, refer back to the chapter on power words). Simplify the communication. Understand the "less is more" rule. We believe in the wisdom that one needs to "be brief, be bright, and be gone." In other words, be concise and interesting and trust that's enough. The less you say, the more people around you will listen when you do have something to say.

Boring: Misjudge What Others Need and Want to Hear

The signs are there, but you might not be paying attention. Employees seem distracted. They look down when you are talking with them, or they take lots of notes. You might think they are listening, but it is exactly the opposite. So, why are you boring them? It is because you are not aware of what they need to know or want to hear? You are not in touch because you are not reading covert messages. You have no clear vision or have not synthesized the information so that your listeners understand how it applies to them. Perhaps you are completely disregarding what people need to hear and instead are paying attention to what you want to say.

Interesting: Wow People with Relevant Content

Don't tell people what you want to tell them. Tell them what they need to know to contribute to the organization, improve their performances, and get themselves to higher levels in the company. Share your vision, tell a relevant story or personal experience, and offer powerful illustrations. Pretend you are the person listening, and picture that person saying, "What's in it for me?" Make sure your content flows logically, and use lots of great examples to clarify the point. Pick out a few "wow" statistics to bolster your message. Speak authentically from your own passion and experience to inspire those listening. Offer clear directions, solutions, and information that will empower your listeners.

Boring: Dull Meetings

Nothing is worse than being trapped in a boring meeting. The leader drones on and on. There is no end in sight, and people are falling asleep from lack of engagement. Others are looking at the clock and thinking about the work waiting at their desks while they waste time in a boring meeting. The leader takes an hour to accomplish what could have been done in ten minutes. Most have been in these boring meetings before, and people dread them. In this YouTube era, everyone wants to be entertained—perhaps too much so. However, the reality is you are competing with many fun, interesting, captivating outlets. In the face of all this entertainment, people expect leaders to have exceptional skills for presenting business concepts, vision, and strategy. The bar has been raised because of the virtual and technical world we live in, and leaders must rise to the challenge of communicating quickly and effectively.

Interesting: Interaction

Shake up the agenda, and always put the most interesting topics at the front. Don't try to shove everything into a meeting. Don't rehash print reports. Don't go on beyond the time you really need just to fill the time slot. Don't conduct every meeting the same way.

Do break the information up into digestible doses, and present those in creative ways. Keep it moving. Encourage participation. Do something surprising to delight and encourage others. Use visuals and ask questions to engage others. Show enthusiasm and energy. Try some creative ideas such as meetings with everyone standing. We've seen leaders use this technique to keep people alert and meetings brief. There are many creative ways to conduct effective meetings, and you can find suggestions through an Internet search.

Boring: Lack of Enthusiasm

If you are not enthusiastic about your company or your work, others will realize it. If you speak in a monotone voice, lack facial expression, or don't have energy, you are seen as disinterested. If you are not interested, why should employees care? If you are late to meetings, are not prepared for meetings, or don't follow through with initiatives, you will be viewed as ineffective or irrelevant. Sometimes senior leaders commit these leadership errors in the mistaken view that seniority gives them the right to relax standards for themselves. Nothing could be further from the truth. No one wants to work under a leader who lacks enthusiasm and engagement.

Interesting: Passion

You must display passion and enthusiasm. Your face and body language should be welcoming. You don't need to be the Energizer Bunny, but you do need to have a certain level of energy about you. Body language speaks volumes, and yours must be energetic and engaged. Lean forward instead of back in your chair. Use eye contact, smile, and affirm others when they contribute. Arrive at meetings early, be prepared, and conduct meetings on time and on task. People respond to the example a leader sets; make sure yours is a good one.

To be an effective leader, you cannot be boring. You must have a personal style or brand that engages others. A great deal has been written about brand. Much of it focuses on superficial things, though, such as appearance. In fact, personal branding is about how you take what you are and what you believe and market that to others. That means you do not act or substantially alter your style. Most people have experienced working with inauthentic leaders. It's obvious the people they are pretending to be are not their real selves. There are many reasons people act, but it is never an effective way to lead.

If you are a reserved person, you might never be outrageously outgoing or a person who attracts attention. That does not mean you cannot find your own style. Also, if you are outgoing, that does not guarantee you have style. You might just be loud. Wherever you are on your leadership journey, you can enhance your style and be more interesting, and here are a few steps to help you get there.

Look the Part

Of course, you must dress appropriately and look the part. Over the years, numerous studies have shown the effect of attractiveness in the workplace. Some studies have concluded that attractive people earn more and get more opportunities. That might or might not be true in a specific workplace. However, we do know that dress contributes to how you are viewed. Dress indicates either a concern or lack of concern for your work. In a corporate casual environment, you should still dress in a contemporary manner and have your own look. A good rule of thumb is to dress at or slightly above the level of your employees and colleagues.

Maintain a Positive Physical Presence

Your physical presence says a lot about your confidence. Some women tend to make themselves look physically small. They shrink into their environments. They hunch their shoulders with their heads forward. They put their hands in their laps with their knees together and feet under their chairs. However, as a leader, it is important to command space. Make yourself larger by holding your head up, sitting up straight, draping an arm over a chair, or putting your hands on the table. Think about a person you know who walks into a room and attracts everyone's attention. What are they doing? They smile. They use the space around them. They gesture. There are a number of studies that point to physical attributes such as height as predictors of success. You might not be tall, but you can command attention by walking with confidence and standing tall.

Express Interest in Others

Finally, you are more interesting when you are interested in others. If your conversation is always about you, that is boring. Engage others by asking these questions:

- What's most important to you?
- What did you mean by that?
- Can you explain why you are having challenges with this situation?
- What did you do that gave us such great results?

Think about people who have great style. Gwen Stefani is the well-known judge from *The Voice*. She is a unique, talented person and a great communicator. She has style. Donald Trump, like him or not, has style. They are memorable people who have found their unique styles. They haven't tried to be copies of others.

It's hard to pinpoint exactly what makes a leader interesting, but people know boring when they see it. If you want to be a great leader, stop being boring. Start leading with style.

Tips and Takeaways:

- To lead with style, you must identify what makes you stand out from others.
- Develop your personal story. Try it out on trusted colleagues to get their reactions.
- Dress in a contemporary style.
- Be enthusiastic.

CHAPTER 20

CONSIDER A LEADERSHIP COACH

I t has become a pretty widely accepted idea that everyone needs professional help from time to time, and this can be especially true in your professional life. Whether you need some guidance on how to handle situations in the workplace, take a promotion, change course, plan your career path, or a host of other challenges, an outside perspective and objective counsel can be valuable. Our experience is that a coach's services can help you grow in ways a mentor's services might not be able to offer.

Both coaches and mentors can add value to your professional career development. Each provides different benefits and challenges you should consider. You must determine which you need and the timing of when you need outside help to best reach your career goals.

You should understand there is a big difference between mentors and coaches. A mentor will help you learn what you need to do. A coach will help you discover why and how to move forward. It is certainly important to understand what to do in your industry and position. This will help you become more competent in your job performance and move forward in your career. A mentor in your field or company can help you learn this important information. In contrast, a coach will dig deeper to help you plot a course for the future according to your passions, talents, life circumstances, and goals. A coach will ask questions to help you think more deeply and understand yourself and what is important to you. A coach will also help you determine if your goals are aligned with your values.

How do you determine if you need a mentor or coach? When is one or the other appropriate? What are the benefits of each choice? As you read more about each resource, you might realize you will need both—simultaneously or separately—at various stages of career growth. Your decision to choose one or the other is an important part of your strategic career plan.

A mentor is generally an experienced professional who offers help to a less-experienced person. A mentor is not usually compensated for his or her time. Many companies have very well-defined mentoring programs that match people based on personality, type of work, and other criteria. In formal programs, a mentor commits to spending a certain amount of time each week or month and holds the mentee accountable for progress. Some mentoring programs have groups of individuals or classes of mentees who take seminars together. Individual one-on-one work supplements these. Generally the candidates selected for these programs are identified as rising stars in the company. They are the high-potential professionals who will be fast-tracked into management. Gaining a mentor from your own company has been an accepted way to help move up the ladder, and for many it works.

An important consideration is that working with a mentor essentially places you in a relationship where you are dependent on someone else's goodwill. If your mentor is busy, as most successful professionals are, he or she might have limited time to contribute to your development. Anticipate the possibility of canceled appointments as your mentor's schedule changes or work emergencies arise. Know that when you work with a mentor, you will get what that mentor has time for, and often a busy mentor does not have the amount of time available that you might need or want. You will be depending on your mentor to advise, facilitate, and navigate your future, and he or she might or might not provide what you need.

Although mentors certainly have value, your mentor might contribute only part of what you need to advance your career. If your mentor is not a strong advocate, you might not progress as quickly as someone who has a stronger advocate. If your mentor leaves the company, you are set adrift. If your mentor is busy and can't devote much time to helping your career, you are frustrated and left without the advice you need. If your mentor is not a good fit for you or inexperienced in mentoring, you might not receive important and necessary help. If your mentor is from your company, he or she might not be impartial. Your mentor could be, knowingly or unknowingly, advising in the company's best interest but not yours.

We believe a mentoring program is a great way to bridge the gap between you and upper management, but you should be thoughtful and strategic about what's in your best interest if you want to advance your career. Be sure to stay in the driver's seat by evaluating your ongoing needs and finding the resources to keep moving forward. Successful professionals continually assess their changing needs for career advancement and find the resources needed to meet those needs.

There are also less-formal mentoring situations where professionals ask people whom they admire to mentor them. They might meet from time to time to discuss issues or questions. In this case, the mentor helps someone out of a desire to give back. Often mentors talk about giving their time because people did it for them. However, because they are doing this for free, they will be limited in the time they can devote. Another consideration is that mentors might be well meaning, accomplished, and successful, but that does not mean they are skilled and have the necessary tools to help people advance their careers. They might offer snippets of helpful information but not comprehensive plans.

To improve basic leadership skills, some professionals take advantage of group leadership programs. A third party such as a chamber of commerce or other organization might run these. They are generally fee-based and can vary widely in content and value. It depends on the facilitator. While this might be a good place to gain general knowledge about leadership skills and practices, it does not replace a comprehensive strategic career plan. Your leadership and career goals will change over time. Your life situation and needs will change too, and it is important to continually assess your needs for personal development.

Failure to assess your needs for personal development can lead to feeling to powerless at work. Women in this situation try to move into the ranks of leadership but just cannot seem to get ahead. Some women might begin to whine that no one notices them or offers chances to contribute more to their organizations. However, successful professionals of either gender must learn to identify the unseen barriers and figure out how to navigate them to advance their careers. Your workplace is not likely to change very much, so it is your responsibility to figure out how to achieve your career goals. Ask yourself, "If nothing changes in my workplace, what is my strategy to get where I want to go? Is this the right company, the right industry, or the right job position for me? How do I plan so I can best utilize my individual talents and passions and stay true to my values?"

This is where a coach can play an important role.

If you need a personalized approach and individual attention, you should consider a coach. A coach is very different from a mentor. A coach is a neutral person who is completely devoted to you and working in your best interests—regardless of the path. A skilled coach has training and certifications. The range of training programs and certifications are vast, and you will need to do your due diligence to determine which ones are important to you. You should interview a coach just as you would any other business resource. You need to ask your potential coach specific questions such as:

- What certifications do you have?
- Is your practice primarily aimed at women? (If yes, you might want to probe further. A good coach can coach both men and women and is more interested in the person than the gender of the client. Is the practice aimed at women because of specific passion or experience? If so, this could be valuable to you as you face situations unique to women.)
- What does your ideal client look like?
- What do you hope to achieve for your clients?
- What can I expect about your coaching process? How often and how long is each session? What is the cost?
- What is the focus of your practice? Are you a life coach, a business coach, or a consultant? (If you are looking for a business focus and the potential coach is focused on building life skills, it might not be a good match.)
- What practical business leadership experience do you have?
- Have you been a CEO, COO, or CFO?
- Have you been the board chair of an organization?

Coaches who have been down in the trenches will have more realistic approaches to the issues you face and broader ranges of tools to assist. Many coaches have extensive education but little real-world experience. While some might argue that these coaches are just as capable as business professionals-turned-coaches, we disagree. There is no substitute for living the day-to-day experience of leading an organization, making the tough decisions, and having to live with the consequences.

How Do You Find a Coach?

Asking professionals you know for a recommendation is a good place to start. To find a coach, you might consider a carefully crafted inquiry to a specific group of people you respect. Never do this in a public forum such LinkedIn or Facebook. Send individual e-mails or make phone calls to professionals you trust. Most coaches gain new clients through word-of-mouth recommendations from current or previous clients for whom coaching made a positive difference.

You can also search for a coach by using local organizations or the Internet. Note the training and certification a coach has achieved. Organizations such as Coach University, Inc., and the International Coaching Federation have high standards. Their training programs are designed to provide the foundation for great coaching. You should ask about the courses your potential coach has taken. A number of reputable national organizations also provide certification. Check them out, and understand the kind of training your coach has taken before you make a commitment.

What can you expect a coach will help you accomplish?

Good coaches go deeper than what you say. They help get to the core of who you are, what you want, and why. They are able to help you turn on the light bulb of discovery. To do that, they must adhere to a code of ethics. The work of a coach is not necessarily telling you what you want to hear. It is about helping you honestly assess your skills and understanding what you need to do to accomplish your goals.

Coaches can also help you face the truth. That might mean understanding that you are not ready to apply for the promotion or lead an organization. Sometimes people think they want to lead, but their actions say otherwise. By asking authentic, direct questions, a coach will help you achieve a greater understanding of your situation. A coach might help you see that you are chasing the wrong thing. For example, you might think you want to lead an organization, but what you really want is more power in your personal life. In that case, you need to make a course correction.

There should never be a time where you feel the coach is sending you covert messages or that the coach is guiding you in one direction or another. You should always feel the coach has your best interests at heart and is concerned about your welfare. The coaching relationship is always about you. Your coach is a person you can depend on. He or she is entirely in your corner with no personal agenda, and anything discussed in a coaching session is completely confidential. You should always feel safe with and supported by your coach.

Now, let's assume you have done your homework, and you found several coaches who have the qualifications you need. How do you narrow it down? One thing you might do is find out how the coach will measure your progress. Ask how long the coach thinks it will take for you to see that progress. The timeframe depends on what you need to do. If you have a very specific issue at work that you are looking to resolve you might need four to six sessions. If you are considering a major life change or have an extremely complex situation it will take longer. Here is a word of caution. Occasionally, a coaching relationship becomes unhealthy because you become dependent on the coach...and the coach lets that happen. In this case, the coaching goes on for years, and the progress is slow. A good coach will push you to take responsibility. The coach can and should help you create ideas and strategies to help you reach your goals. Unlike a therapist who helps you sort out the past, a coach will help you focus on the future. If the past is standing in the way, then you might need a therapist. However, if you want help with future career moves, then look for a coach. In summary, a coach should:

- Start with a focus on what you want to achieve.
- Help identify the work to be done.

- Help you access your skills.
- Help create homework and actionable strategies to achieve your goals.
- Measure progress and hold you accountable.
- Help you create a path for the future.
- Wrap up and turn you loose.

Hiring a coach is an investment in your future, but cost can be an obstacle. Some businesses will pay for a coach. If your company offers that benefit, should you take advantage? Maybe. Maybe not. If your business is paying for the coach, your work with that coach is shaped by what will benefit the organization. The business wants to develop leaders who will help the organization move ahead. That just makes good business sense. If you believe the company is a good fit for your future and a place where you can advance your career, then you might feel comfortable with the coach they select.

On the other hand, if you have doubts about your long-term commitment to the company, then you might want to personally pay an independent coach who will be concerned purely with your interests. The costs can vary, but remember this is a business decision. Just as you would invest in a personal trainer to help you get fit faster, a business coach can help you move ahead into a leadership position more quickly.

In summary, should you choose a mentor or a coach?

A mentor can be a wonderful gift, but you get what you pay for. You will be dependent upon the mentor's goodwill and time availability. If you need a little advice occasionally, this could be an option. However, if you truly want to take control of your career, the idea of waiting for your company to provide you a mentor puts you in a dependent position instead of empowering you to get what you need when you need it. You could be wasting valuable time and missing opportunities. By carefully choosing a competent coach and accessing that coach at critical times in your career, you can achieve greater responsibility, a higher salary, and a quicker return on your investment. Taking control of your career in this way puts you in the driver's seat and empowers you to break through invisible barriers that might be in the way.

Tips and Takeaways:

- There are big differences between a coach and a mentor. You should determine which you need and the timing of when you need help to best reach your career goals.
- An outside perspective and objective counsel can be valuable at critical decision points in your career.
- Do your homework to vet a potential coach, and be sure to ask the coach specific questions.

CHAPTER 21

KNOW WHEN TO CHANGE COURSE AND EVOLVE

E very leader knows that leadership is complex and dynamic, and great leaders do not keep doing the same things over and over. To lead effectively, you must be able to change course and evolve. You must also develop self-awareness so you can determine when and how to evolve. You must have the confidence to step into new situations, try new things, and be open to new possibilities. Knowing when and how to make effective changes can be tricky.

We've provided six common signs to help you determine if change should be considered. If you recognize your situation in any of these descriptions, look at the tips and suggestions on how to adapt and evolve through them to gain greater respect and trust in your leadership.

1. Recurring problems

There are moments in tough situations when you think, "I have been here before. I have dealt with this same problem in the past." It could be an employee issue. Perhaps it is a problem with a customer. It might be an infrastructure problem. Whatever the situation, if you find yourself consistently having to go back to deal with basic issues, then you should consider that you have not solved the fundamental or core problem.

Suggestions:
If you are facing a difficult situation, we suggest asking yourself some probing questions:

- Have I done a good job of understanding the situation and determining what needs to be permanently put in place? Is this an isolated incident or symptom of a more pervasive problem?
- Do I have a strategic plan, and have I communicated it properly?
- Is the plan or corrective action ineffective? Do I need to change the plan?
- Is my team trained and capable of executing the plan?
- Am I the cause of this situation? Can I make the necessary changes, or do I need outside help or coaching?

One of the most important things to do in a difficult situation is maintain a positive outlook, but this can be the most difficult time to be positive. Nonetheless, a leader's job is to be proactive and positive—especially in the face of difficulty. If a situation is bad because of particular team members, then you might need to make some difficult choices. One might be to remove these individuals from the workplace. Other options can be to more clearly communicate targets and goals or retrain team members.

Cynthia offered the following example of a difficult situation in the workplace. An employee working at her company when it was a two-person operation was unable to adapt and make the transition as the organization grew. In the early days, "Mary" was a model employee. She was responsive, attentive, and organized. As time went on, she became increasingly unable to work with customers and was disruptive. Her attitude was harming customer relationships and the company culture. Cynthia began spending more and more time managing the bad behavior of this employee and less time doing the important work of leading the organization forward. Worst of all, it was beginning to negatively affect other employees. It became clear it was time for "Mary" to go, and Cynthia fired her. It was the obvious and only possible resolution for this tense situation. While no leader likes to take this drastic action, it is important that harmful situations be dealt with swiftly. This is in the best interest of the entire organization.

2. You Run on Autopilot

Predictability can be good in some situations, but if your colleagues and employees always know how you will react, what you will say, and what decisions you will make, then you might be stuck in a rut. You might be acting out old, tired patterns instead of assessing the current situation and making thoughtful and timely decisions. You might not be aware of how conditions are changing in your organization and industry. This approach can demotivate everyone on your team and stall innovation and creativity.

Suggestions:

If people always know how you will react, then you might need to make a conscious effort to challenge yourself to think differently. Look back at some decisions you have made in the last year. See if there is a pattern of approaching problems with standard solutions, processes, and answers. If you find there is a pattern that is holding you back, it is time to take action. If you have always used the same advisors, perhaps you need to expand your network. If you have always used the same decision-making process, try something new. There is a difference between being a stable, reasonable decision-maker and falling into the trap of doing the same old thing. Know the difference so you can make the appropriate changes. Ask yourself these questions to do a self-assessment:

- Am I concerned about what others will say about me, so I play it safe and do the same things over and over?
- Am I afraid to try a new approach because I might fail?
- Are my patterns of behavior moving me toward my goals or keeping me from attaining them?
- Do I make decisions based on the past or where I want the organization to be in the future?

This is a good time to go back and reread the chapter "Be a Strategic Thinker." Think about ramping up your curiosity by questioning what you assume or think you know. Remember to ask questions that get at the "why" and "how" of what you are doing. Don't assume you already understand a situation. Embrace the idea that you might need to create some new patterns of behavior. You won't be able to do it right away. Research shows it takes between eighteen and 224 days to make changes. Of course, people who are highly motivated to make changes can do amazing things in short periods of time.

3. You Are Out of Touch

It's important for a leader to be able to feel and understand the heartbeat of his or her organization. What makes it tick? What efforts excite and inspire the work? What helps people connect the dots between their work and the strategic objectives of the company? Leaders are not lone wolves. If you find your actions are disjointed from the efforts of others or your thinking does not align with the organization, then you might be out of sync. As a result, you might not be as effective as you should be.

Suggestions:
If you are frequently butting heads with colleagues and feeling you are the lone voice on an issue, you need to change your position. Try to assess why you are out of sync with the rest of the organization. Ask yourself these questions:

- Do you have a different perspective? If so, have you taken time to understand the perspectives of other team members?
- Do you want to go down a different path than others, and is there support for your ideas?
- Can you determine if your ideas require an overhaul?
- Have you observed the covert behavior of team members toward your ideas? What do their reactions tell you?

In order to be in sync with your organization, you must do two important things: listen and participate. People spend a significant amount of time talking in the workplace and far too little time listening. Good listening skills can be developed, but you must be aware of your perceptions and work hard to remain neutral. How you perceive a person influences what you hear. If you believe the person doesn't have enough experience, you might dismiss a potentially great idea. If you misunderstand what a person is saying or you jump ahead too quickly to a conclusion, you might miss important information. Listening helps improve communication and shows you respect others. Listening will help you get in sync with what others are thinking.

One thing to note—if you are a creative thinker in a company that cannot think creatively, you might never be in sync. In this case, reassess your fit in the company. Consider realigning with a company that shares your passions, values, and creative approach.

STOP WISHING. STOP WHINING. START LEADING.

4. Your Network Is Ineffective

While many people think they understand networking and believe they have built extensive networks, it just might not be true. A functional and effective network is one that connects you with others for the purpose of getting things done. Your network should help you navigate the complexities of your organization, make connections, and help the organization become stronger as a whole. Sometimes you assist your network, and other times your network helps you. The network members provide access to senior leaders. They help you get your ideas recognized. They open opportunities for new business vendors or customers. They help problem solve and provide resources when you face challenges. If you find your network letting you down when you reach out, then you need to reevaluate your network and develop some new contacts.

Suggestions:
Think about why your network is ineffective. Perhaps your network consists of great contacts, but you have failed to utilize them. In that case, be more proactive about setting goals and connecting with your network to help achieve your goals.

Consider if you have been intentional about developing a strong network or have just connected with people who happened to cross your path. If it's the latter, think about what industries you should connect with and which positions in those industries. Then place yourself in situations with opportunities to meet these people. This could be anything from a conference to chamber of commerce networking events to trade shows. The list is endless.

Regardless of who you meet, the first and most important way to connect with people is to help them first and be genuine about it. Nobody likes a new "friend" who is only out to get something. Take a real interest in new contacts. Find out about their businesses and their positions in their businesses. Do you know people you can connect them with who will help them reach their goals? If you have a heartfelt interest in other people, building and maintaining a great network will be enjoyable and rewarding.

Develop relationships with your contacts by sending congratulatory messages on their accomplishments. Send holiday a greeting, or just get together occasionally to catch up. Be sure you develop a diverse network. Include people you perceive as different than yourself. You never know where a connection might lead in the future, and a diverse network will help you grow personally and in your leadership journey.

5. Your Workplace Is Hostile

The work environment is a living, breathing thing. People hope that the work they do is valued and they are trusted to lead their organizations. However, conditions can change. Perhaps you work for a company that is experiencing transitions at the highest levels—in the boardroom or the C-suite. Maybe another organization acquired or merged with your company. You start to notice that promises are made but not kept. You begin to sense there are secrets within the organization, and you are not in the know. Your decisions are being challenged or (worse) ignored. This environment is no longer friendly to you or your efforts to lead, and that is a signal you need to assess the core of the problem and your options.

Suggestions:

If a work environment is hostile, it affects your entire life—not just your work. To lead effectively, it is important you are trusted and valued by the organization. Ask yourself these questions:

- Is this really a hostile environment, or are there simply disagreements that are not being properly expressed?

- Am I misinterpreting the actions of others? Am I being overly sensitive?
- Do I believe the organization is working against me? Do I actually have some evidence that supports this?
- Has the company philosophy or culture changed?
- Have people lost faith in my ability to lead? Is this tied to a specific action?
- Are team members resisting my leadership style? If so, how do I need to grow?

If you determine that the environment is hostile due to circumstances beyond your control, you have two options. Neither will be easy. If you believe the organization is a good fit for you in the long run, then you might need to rethink your behavior or leadership. You must be willing to listen to messages from others that are not easy to hear. You might be correct in your position on an issue, but you might not have done the work to solicit input to see if there are other things you should take into account. Let's say you want to restructure your team because there are problems with efficiency. You announce a plan to move some individuals into other areas and bring in new team members. You did this without getting input. You get pushback because the reason the team is not efficient has more to do with lacking the proper tools to communicate. The team gets hostile because you did not seek input or support for the changes. This situation actually occurs frequently. Cynthia has seen this time and time again in her work with corporations. The approach negatively affects team morale, and sometimes valuable team members leave the company as a result.

Effective leaders give others the time and attention to provide input and adapt to changes. Once you do this, you might find that the barriers can be overcome, and the team can move effectively forward together.

For example, one of Cynthia's clients was working to develop a new product. This company made components for the industry but never an entire system. The company's leader felt strongly that they needed to provide a product and moved ahead to develop it. The company spent significant time and money on the new product and the launch. While the product did well initially, the organization's most-senior leaders did not see the value. The leader began to see her decisions being questioned. The budget for advertising was reduced. The leader found she was the target of negative comments, and the environment turned hostile. The result was that the leader was forced out.

Hostility in the workplace exists for many reasons. It can be because of a difference of opinion or style or something more sinister. If the hostility in your workplace stems from harassment, violence, or other dysfunctional behaviors, it is probably time to look for a new job in a more healthy culture. There are workplace regulations that cover harassment, violence, and other behavior, but because these behaviors are often subtle, legal action might be difficult to pursue.

6. You Are Bored

After you have led an organization for a lengthy time, you might discover you are simply not as excited about the work, the people, or the customers. It happens, and there is nothing wrong with it. You might be in a place where you have achieved everything you can or want in your position. You might need a new challenge. You might feel trapped and not able to grow professionally because your organization is not as progressive as you would like. You might have just outgrown the job—even if it is at the highest level of the organization. You might be a big fish in a little pond, and you need a bigger pond. Perhaps the organization was not a good fit in the first place. Whatever the reason, you are not getting the satisfaction you need and want from this position of leadership.

You start to dread going to work and watch the clock while you are there.

All these signs point to the possibility that it is time to make a change and evolve. This does not necessarily mean you will need to leave your position, but if you cannot resolve the issues standing in your way, it should be one of the options on the table.

Change is difficult, so expect this to feel scary or confusing. It will take thought and energy, but know that change also brings new opportunities. One way to move forward is to address the issue directly. You can't hide because the issues won't go away, and they might actually intensify.

Career change (like every business endeavor) must be strategic. You must stop and think first about the big picture. You must gather information and then really analyze what needs to be changed. This is a time when you might benefit from a few sessions with a leadership coach or a talk with a mentor who knows you well. You might also consider reaching out to your network of leaders. They have probably faced change before and acted on it. Fresh ears and eyes on your situation can bring clarity to what changes you should make as well as possible strategies. Share information with your advisors, and chart your reasons for contemplating change. Once you have developed the big-picture plan, you can begin working on goals and time lines.

Suggestions:
Even the most exciting job can be boring at times. The first questions to ask are:

- Why are you bored?
- Are you doing work you should no longer be doing?
- Are you in a stagnated organization?

- Have you lost your passion for the work?
- Has the business changed, and you simply are not excited about the direction?

In the past, leaders stayed at the tops of their organizations for many years without much thought. Today, that is much less prevalent and leaders sometimes make changes for the wrong reasons. Before you make a change, you should understand why you are bored. It might be that you have not developed your team so you are stuck doing the same work repetitively. If that is the case, start to train others so you can free up time to take on new challenges. If the organization is in a rut, how can you innovate and introduce fresh ideas? It could be by creating a new product or service. Perhaps it's a push to identify new customers or employees. However, it might just be time for a new personal challenge by finding a new opportunity.

An effective leader knows when to change course and evolve and does not wait until the signs are flashing neon. They are self-aware and proactive about creating futures for themselves and their organizations.

Tips and Takeaways:

- Be alert for signs that a change is needed.
- You must be aware of people's actions and reactions to get a good understanding of the workplace.
- Communication skills, especially listening, are critical to determine if you are in sync with your organization.
- Change is difficult. It can take between 18 and 224 days to change a behavior pattern.

A Few Final Thoughts

We did not want to leave you without a few closing thoughts. Opportunities for women exist today as never before. Perhaps they don't exist in every company, but they do exist in greater abundance than ever in history. If you only see barriers for women in your company, we urge you to begin looking for an organization that does provide leadership opportunities for women. There are now more female entrepreneurs than ever. The climate for women business owners is ripe with opportunity. Whatever the course you choose, make no mistake - success won't be handed to you just as it was not handed to us. You will need to earn your way at every step.

Based on our experience, we have tried to offer practical examples of what to do and what to avoid if you aspire to lead. We have tried to provide tools and to encourage you to be thoughtful about the level of leadership you wish to achieve and the timing of your career decisions. Some might read what we've written and interpret some of the messages as harsh. This does not offend us, and we don't apologize to those who would judge straightforward messages as harsh. Ironically, being offended has been a significant barrier for women to advance in leadership because the attitude inhibits growth. Women will lead most effectively when they get past personal feelings and embrace hard truths.

We challenge women to be on guard against complaining, whining, or wanting to be rescued. We also suggest you give a wide berth to people who tend to rescue you or make excuses for you. They might actually be disempowering you from becoming the leader you could be.

We encourage you to seek relationships with other great leaders who will challenge you and hold you accountable. We know women are strong and resilient when they resolve to be. We know women are capable of amazing leadership when those around them expect the best and don't let them off the hook. That is why our message might seem harsh. It is also why we feel compelled to talk straight. We did not want to soften these leadership lessons to appeal to everyone. This book is not for everyone. It is specifically for women who choose to lead beyond the home into local, national, and international leadership.

We hope you will refer to this book often as you face new challenges on your career journey. We challenge you to believe in yourself and keep going when you face discouragement. We hope our experiences inspire you to do so.

We are not extraordinary women. We've just exercised extraordinary perseverance and determination, and you can too. Our highest desire is to empower women to become the leaders our world needs now and in the future. We hope you will be one of them!